Beyond
MY STORY
Within

BRIAN DARDEN

Beyond My Story Within

Copyright © 2024 by Brian Darden. All rights reserved.

Editing, book design, and cover design by Next Page Editing & Design (itsthenextpage.com)

Cover and interior photos provided by Brian Darden.

ISBN: 979-8-218-40547-2

All rights reserved. No part of this publication may be reproduced, stored in any retrieval system, or transmitted in any form or by any means electronic, mechanical, photocopying, recording, or otherwise without the prior written consent of the author.

This book is a memoir. It reflects the author's present recollections of experiences over time. Some events have been compressed, and some dialogue has been recreated.

Contents

Appreciation i

Introduction vii

PART 1: The Family That Raised Me 1

1. The Journey 2
2. Behind My Smile 7
3. Abandoned by My Father, but God 9
4. Despised by My Mother, but God 17
5. Abused by My Older Brother, but God 27
6. The Benefit 38
7. A Sprinkle of Love 40
8. Making Sense of It All 44

PART 2: The Family That Grew Me 46

9. The Man Who Stood in the Gap 47
10. A Coach's Impact 52
11. Growing Despite Thorns and Weeds 54
12. The Reminder 58
13. Still Destined 63
14. The Loaded Question 67
15. Moving On 73
16. Appreciation for Where I'm From 76

PART 3: The Family That Loves Me 79

17. Appreciating My Wife 80
18. Putting Her First 84
19. My Pet Peeve 86
20. Not My Car 88

21. Meeting Her Needs 90
22. The Storm 92
23. A Mother's Love 100
24. The Apology 105

PART 4: A Family Learning from the Past 108

25. The Family Effect 109
26. My Children 119
27. A Season to Remember 122
28. Forgiveness in Action 134
29. Closure and Relief 143
30. Redirection 145

PART 5: From My Family to Yours 148

31. Helping Others 149
32. Crossing the Bridge 151
33. Learning to Love Yourself 156
34. Looking in the Mirror 158
35. Wise Council 161
36. Embracing Leadership 164
37. Knowing Our Parents 168
38. Education Matters 173
39. Beyond My Internal Ceiling 176
40. In Conclusion 179

My Prayer 182

The Power of Change 183

Epilogue: Next Chapter TBD 184

About the Author 187

Appreciation

Today, I choose to be the authentic, energized, and unapologetic version of myself with an appreciation for the struggles of my past that have become my strengths. Even those moments I thought I wouldn't survive have become a snapshot of God's grace and mercy as I realize that someone has always shown up just in time to provide the help I need.

First, I thank God for His saving power. I thank my mother for making the decision to bring me into this world because I would not be here without her choice to be my mother. Much appreciation also goes out to the father figures who showed up when I needed them the most in the absence of my own father.

To the coaches who filled the gap of support in my life

when I needed it the most, which starts with Coach Doug Baggett, known to me as "The Man Who Stood in the Gap," the first coach to pour into my life. Coach Baggett saw the good in me beyond my struggles and gave me the opportunity to be a part of his baseball team and eventually his basketball team. He showed up in my life when I thought it was about to end because my care for life was fading and I assumed something bad was going to happen. As Coach Baggett overlooked my struggle, he began to expose me to the simple things in life beyond the chaos I was living in, like a trip to a local restaurant for a hamburger and fries and dessert. Those moments were life-changing for me, and the only thing he wanted in return was for me to succeed in life. Coach also took me fishing, which allowed me to see life with different scenery. When you are on the water in a boat, things slow down, and you get a chance to appreciate the wind and the waves. Coach gave me hope and support; because of the difference he made in my life, I have the drive to do the same for others. I thank God for Coach Doug Baggett; he will always be a father of influence to me, and I love him to life.

To Coach K and in remembrance of Coach Moore, who had no idea what I was going through at home but knew something wasn't right, so they simply provided the things I needed. I would never ask for anything and would go without food as long as I could wear my uniform. I thank God for the nuggets of wisdom, love, and support they gave me. I think my story came to life for them on senior night when I had no family support and the coach's wife escorted me while my teammates had their parents. I was the leading scorer and rebounder on the team and was driven to win because it meant everything to me—the team had become my family since I had no parental support.

To Coach Underwood, who covered me while I was in the transitional period from a young man to manhood. I made many mistakes and needed a chance to grow through those mistakes, and he was there to see me through with support and protection from some of my immature actions.

To Coach Daniel, who saw a father coaching his son and a team of players who also needed a father figure. Coach Daniel mentored me as a coach on how important it is to push the players to get an education. That mentoring led me to coaching and winning a State Championship and going 8-1 in the 2007 14&Under AAU National Tournament, finishing seventh in the country out of a hundred sixty teams. I became his head assistant coach at the high school level, where we continued to win. My son received more than twenty college scholarship offers, and six other players from our team who were academically prepared for college also received scholarship offers. Together, we won two district titles and had a state tournament appearance.

To Coach Joyner, who allowed me to continue the journey with my son as a coach and father. Just when I thought I would be a parent in the stands, Coach extended the opportunity for me to be one of his assistant coaches as a mentoring coach. While I welcomed the opportunity, I didn't want to crowd my son's space during his college journey, so I asked my son what he thought about me being one of his coaches, and he said that he would love to have me there, so I guess it was a done deal.

What a ride it was! That coaching position allowed me to mentor the players and be more of a father than a coach during this season. I thank God for this journey of fatherhood as it has given me the opportunity to be the father I yearned for as a young man to many and, most of all, my own son. When he went to Hampton University, he won two MEAC Championships, one regular season championship, and made two NCAA appearances. Only God could have created such an outcome.

As an adult, my wife, Kimberly, has been my rock and pillow as she encouraged me to accept the idea of leading others, my brother-in-love has shown me what family support should look like, and my mother-in-love has provided much-needed guidance and nurturing. To my pops who has given me his story as an adult, my sister who continues to say, "keep doing your thing, little brother," my children who encourage me to keep grinding and growing, and my former neighbors and friends who helped change my views and influenced me to adjust my actions.

To Lisa, who would not allow me to stay in the background as a leader at work and took it upon herself to push me out of the shadows and seek mentors on a senior manager level. She pulled me up the leadership mountain with the assignment to do the same for others. This gave me the opportunity to learn and lead on another level. To the leaders who provided mentorship and the opportunity to learn from their personal journeys, thank you for giving me a chance to grow as a leader.

To Troy, who heard my heart and saw the leader in me the first time we met and accepted my request for mentorship. He was the key that unlocked my potential as a leader; his greatest message to me has been to remove the limitations I have placed on myself, lead others with love, and operate with no fear. He also reminded me of the fact that God is for me, so what other people think of me is none of my business. He has influenced me to stand as an unmovable pillar when I know my decision or position on something is right, no matter who questions it. Thank you for your mentorship and, above all, your friendship.

To Stephen, who has become a coach and a friend as

he guides me through the process of learning how to lead others as a senior manager from the heart and not from my head. He is the ultimate example of meeting someone for the first time and walking away from that encounter feeling great about who you are regardless of your past because he leaves you focusing on your future and what you can do with your gifts to lead others in a positive way. Your presence is energetic, and I thank God for you.

To Brian Baker, who asked me that loaded question, provoking me to take a closer look in the mirror, and to the many others God used to tell me that my platform is bigger than my imagination and whose statements have been voices of encouragement. To all the men and women of the gospel who have shared the good news of God's word with me. Thank you to my spiritual leaders for your example and the push to get moving. God Bless!

Introduction

I went from an abandoned infant at six months of age, to a gifted child with the hope of doing something with his life, to an athletic teenager who eventually won championships and MVP awards, to a driven adult who became an arena football player for the Norfolk Nighthawks, to a husband of thirty-three years and counting, to a father of three adult children, to a championship coach at the youth, high school, and college levels, to a grandfather of seven and a servant leader. Getting beyond our story within is the most important journey we will ever take in life. We can allow ourselves to be defeated by our story within or use it as fuel to lead us down a path of relentlessness to be everything we are capable of becoming in life. What we've been through can have a long-lasting effect on our lives in one way or another, influencing our decisions and impacting the results of everything we do.

Should we just forget about the pain of our past? If so, how? If not, why?

It's not easy to just forgive and forget, especially when those painful moments come from the people we should be able to trust, such as our parents and family members.

Many people have said to me, "Don't look back; just press your way forward," and while that is great advice, what I've learned is that I cannot move on to my place of destiny until I am mentally released from the shackles of my past, because those unresolved issues continue to hang around. I learned how to protect the child within me and hide my pain with a smile while struggling to trust others and, above all, trust God.

I listened to others who did not have the same experiences in life tell me how to overcome my struggles. I tried hard to be as strong as I could, but the pain inside me continued to grow, and for the life of me, I could not understand why. It felt at times like I was drowning internally in my own sorrow, experiencing moments of reflection that usually ended with tears rolling down my face. However, in those moments, God would remind me that I am still here and that I have survived for a purpose bigger than my imagination.

After many years of silence, I finally took the advice of

my wife and began to write down all that I could remember. Writing my story became my relief switch, and when I share my story with others, God shows me how these conversations help others overcome their own internal challenges while I experience healing on the inside.

Over the years, I developed a guarded and protective mentality, feeling like I had to be the toughest person in every situation. I shed no tears as a young teenager because I didn't believe they would help me. Those tears didn't help when I was a child, and truth be told, I despised the very thought of crying as a man until now because I now realize it doesn't take away from my manhood at all. I was conditioned by my mother to keep my tears and hurt inside of me, and you *know* I passed this on to my children, but I thank God for my wife, who has always been the balance for our family when it came to these matters.

I recognize that some people do things to help others every chance they get because they remember the moments when they needed help themselves, while some people are driven to hurt others because they've been hurt by someone they trusted and haven't learned how to process that internal pain—thus, they attack others because they assume those people will eventually hurt them as well.

For years, I trusted myself and waited for those

closest to me to cause heartache like my family did when I was growing up. The sad part is the people I was waiting to hurt me as an adult were my wife and children, the very folks who cherish and appreciate me every day.

My wife and I were married for fifteen years before I could begin telling her about some of the things I experienced as a youth. I survived to be a positive example, and my scars have become stars of hope for others. I now strive to be the best I can be in all areas of my life as the authentic, energized, and unapologetic version of myself. I am blessed to be a blessing to others.

Talk about therapy; I would have never thought that by telling my own story, I would experience such relief from the internal pain I've held inside of me for more than twenty years. Although I hate shedding tears, I began to see things differently during those moments of sharing and recognize that I survived all of the adversity I've faced. No matter how hard I fight to hold back my emotions with everything in me, I am unable to contain those tears of relief that flow when I share my story with others.

Some people make it through life with only a few scars, but many people have endured physical and emotional scars that they struggle to overcome, finding themselves in a deep pit or very low valley in life with little to no hope of recovery. But God can deliver us from any situation—I am a living witness and example of His grace and mercy.

I have held onto the hurt long enough, I have been liberated from the judgment of people, and I am no longer held in bondage by anyone else's opinion of me. I accept the call to do my part by sharing my story to free others who may be facing the same challenges in life.

My life has become an open book to many as my wife and I serve other families and married couples by sharing our testimonies, giving messages of hope, and letting them know that they can make it through anything. Each time I tell someone about my life, I gain strength, and my story within becomes **"Tears of Joy."**

My desire is to help others identify and recover from the sources of their internal pain by letting them know they are not alone and that they can overcome anything with the help of God. One of the main points I share with others is the fact that we survived, and with that said, we have a chance to make a difference not only in our lives but in the lives of others as well.

I realize that there are folks who have endured some of the worst acts of cruelty known to mankind, and those willing to tell their stories become hope for others. We typically see that when we tell our stories, we become living proof that you can make it through anything; the key is to believe and be positive and relentless.

My story is not an unfamiliar one, but there aren't many folks willing to tell their stories. The challenges we face in life with internal pain can be overwhelming at times, and some parents become frustrated and angry just trying to make it from one day to the next. This can lead to raising children in a hostile environment, which usually occurs right in the home for most of us who have faced these types of challenges. We become dissatisfied, disappointed, deserted, and desperate, and sometimes depressed, which can become a mental box of limitations for many people that can take a long time and require help to overcome.

We must learn how to move forward with our lives without duplicating the bad actions of our parents. Our parents' mistakes have the potential to be transferred from generation to generation until someone stops transferring the hurt, overcomes their internal pain, and chooses to be better. We cannot love others unconditionally until we learn to love ourselves—and our immediate family members. My hope is to share my story and shift others to soar in their purpose. Let's go, God!

No matter what you've been through, if you still have breath in your body and are still standing, I encourage you to accept the fact that God has a plan for your life, and He is waiting on you to trust Him more than you trust yourself. You shall achieve and reach your destiny if you believe and do things others think are impossible.

PART 1

The Family That Raised Me

CHAPTER 1

The Journey

My journey began as a newborn child in Hampton, Virginia, in 1968. However, the memories of my childhood are from the time we spent in Jamaica, Queens in New York, where I attended elementary and intermediate school before we went back to Virginia in 1982, where I attended York High School for my freshman and sophomore years and Denbigh High School for my junior and senior years. As a youngster, I loved math, and despite going from school to school and dealing with so much adversity, I was an honor roll student all the way through the sixth grade. However, I eventually became very guarded and quiet due to the emotional and physical abuse I was dealing with, which began to affect my desire to apply myself academically.

As a ten-year-old, I was either extremely adventurous or out of my mind because most of the things I did were life-threatening: for example, laying in the gravel between the third rails of the Amtrak train tracks while two trains were passing by in opposite directions. The wind from the trains could have bounced me back and forth between them as they passed one another, but they passed by, and I very carefully got up as my friends at the bottom of the hill were shouting how crazy I was for doing that. What they didn't know was how hard I was praying as I lay there between those passing trains.

Another day, I climbed up the front of our apartment building into the third-floor window, which had to be at least twenty-five feet in the air; this was a moment when someone said, "I dare you," and that's all it took for me to begin my climb up to the third floor. I also climbed out of our apartment window from the second floor more than once and landed in the grass to break my fall. However, the greatest risk I took was the day I walked across an I-beam of a new building under construction that was at least twenty feet off the ground. These are just some of the things I did that were cutting-edge or life-threatening, as the violence in my home caused me to care less and less about life. The protection of God was obviously present in those dangerous moments of my childhood.

In Queens, we lived in Baisley Park Housing, known as "Baisley Projects," which was an environment of adversity with moments of joy because everyone had their own struggles at home that sometimes made their way out into public view. We learned to find ways to have fun, but it didn't take much for things to turn violent because you never knew when someone would reach their limit or feel like they couldn't take the struggles of life anymore. Although we struggled as a family to overcome our issues, I realized that we were not the only ones going through tough times. However, the violence in our home spilled out in the streets when my sister got into a fight with some girls. We ended up needing the support of other families living in the projects when some outsiders came after my sister in our neighborhood. It was a bad day for those girls. Not long after that, my brother was brought home by the police after getting caught vandalizing property in another neighborhood. We also got into a big fight in our neighborhood that had us going against another family and having to involve the support of our older cousins, which did not turn out well for the other family.

Violence had become a normal way of life, and we would see a fight or be in a fight on a weekly basis. I saw people get shot and stabbed at a young age, which impacted my view of life. It seemed like it was just a matter of time before something bad happened that we may not have survived, but God had a better plan.

Now, I must say that intermediate school in New York City was like high school in Virginia as far as what you were exposed to, but New York was on another level. You had to be strong and determined to stay away from bad activities, or you could find yourself going down a path in life that many people cannot recover from without Godly intervention. We were surrounded by drugs and alcohol, normalized violence, and multiple forms of hustling to survive. It seemed like the teachers in New York were authorized to be physical, or they just did it because the kids were physical with the teachers whenever there were altercations. The violence was on a different level; there were times when people fought like it was their last moment in life. The struggle was real.

When I was thirteen, my mother decided to pack up and leave New York, bringing us back to Virginia. Believe it or not, we stayed with my father in Richmond for about two months, but that didn't last long because both of them soon realized why they weren't together in the first place. Of course, we attended another school in Richmond for a short period, and I did get to see my dad for a moment. I actually had a chance to stay with him, but I didn't know or trust him because he left when I was six months old, and unfortunately, all I knew was the chaos I was living in during that period of time.

From there, we ended up in Yorktown, Virginia, of all places. Talk about going through mental shock, going from the city to the suburbs, but it was better than the atmosphere we were in back then.

I mean no disrespect to anyone living there now, but please understand that the violence we were exposed to every day was life-threatening, and at any given moment, things could change for the worse with little to no chance of recovery. When living under those conditions, you don't think about next week or next month because your focus is on surviving the day and making it to the next one. Sometimes, the struggle would be so overwhelming that people would take their own lives. Today, I am thankful that Baisley Projects is a part of my life story; overcoming that season of adversity has led me to value every day and each person I cross paths with.

CHAPTER 2

Behind My Smile

While I am known for smiling all the time, my story begins with a moment of rage.

One Thanksgiving, my mother and father decided to show up at the same time that my wife usually cooks a huge dinner for family and friends. It was rare to have both of my parents in the same space because my mother was still angry with my father after more than forty years. My mother despised the fact that my father and I had a healthy relationship while she and I didn't, so she decided to tell me what happened when I was just an infant.

At six months old, she took me to my father's house, tossed me on his bed, and then said to my father, "Here is your son; now *you* raise him." I guess it was an aggressive toss because she said that my father lost it and began to whip her behind. It was so bad that my grandfather and uncles had to pull him off my mother. She eventually broke away, grabbed me off the bed, and made it to her car, but my father came after her, shattered the window of her car, and continued to beat my mother until he was restrained again, and my mother was able to drive away.

Hearing this story for the first time at the age of forty-two was shocking, to say the least, but it gave me a better understanding of why my mother was so angry and frustrated with my father all these years.

CHAPTER 3

Abandoned by My Father, but God

My father sat at the Thanksgiving table in silence while my mother told the story of him abandoning us. There was no denial of the event as he shook his head in acknowledgment of all that my mother said. My mother was upset while telling the story and raised her voice a little; I guess looking at him while telling the story was like adding fuel to the fire, even more than forty years later. My father did not add to or take away from the story because he recognized my mother's emotions and did not want things to escalate.

I didn't know how to react, so I just listened. My wife was stunned because she had been trying to figure out why I was so disconnected from my parents and siblings for years.

There is always an explanation or an attempt to justify our own actions after we take them. I believe my father decided that self-satisfaction and the pleasure of having other women mattered more than his children, and unfortunately, there are too many of us who go through the experience of being abandoned by our fathers. My father left to get away from my mother and live his own life, free from the responsibility of raising his own children. While separation from my mother may have been a wise choice due to the violence between them, removing himself completely from our lives presented many challenges for my sister and me because he wasn't there to provide the things we needed, prepare us for life, and protect us from danger.

I missed out on guidance from the one man who was supposed to cover me with unconditional love and teach me how to be a man. I spent many days looking out the window, wondering if my father would ever show up to save me from the struggles of life. I had so many feelings of hopelessness, anger, hurt, disappointment, and self-blame that grew inside me over time because I wondered if it was my fault that my father left.

While I felt unprotected and exposed to the many dangers that were everywhere as we grew up in the projects of New York City—where crime and violence were normal parts of life—it was right in my own home where I experienced the abuse from my brother and the rage of my mother that had the greatest impact on me as a child.

When I look back at some of those experiences, I conclude that God is real, and there is no doubt in my mind that God allowed me to survive to be a better person who is committed to making a difference in the lives of others.

My father left me void of the support I needed from him, but God—who supplies all of our needs according to all He possesses, which is everything—covered me with a father's guidance from many directions. I received discipline from my mother's boyfriend in New York from time to time when I did something wrong. I also received guidance from my cousins, my basketball coaches, and a few of my friends' parents, who took the time to share some nuggets of wisdom with me. I still had trust issues, though, because when your parents abandon their role, you have a hard time trusting anyone else (at least right away), which can become a problem. This can lead to learning hard lessons through trial and error because we rely so heavily on ourselves that we disregard the wise counsel that comes our way from others.

As a teenager, I began to think I was my own guide and authority, so I was resistant to the help others were trying to give me. As an abandoned young man, I assumed everyone would treat me the same way my parents did, so it became difficult to believe in the messages coming from those who really cared.

My father went on to marry five other women and played the role of a father to many others while we suffered the hardships of life. Despite the damage done, I have worked hard to be the best I can be as a man of God, husband, father, and mentor to others.

My father's absence made God's divine presence more visible, and as I look back over my life, I can embrace the fact that I've been marked to make a difference.

A father who chooses to be absent will risk losing his voice of reason with his children. My father gave up his voice of reason with me, which caused me to go through a process of building trust as an adult by revisiting tough moments from the past. Our children are exposed to many things, and to guide them in the right direction, we must keep our voice. My father was consumed with satisfying himself and pursued everything else, giving up his right to speak into the lives of his children.

At the end of the day, God would not allow me to have bitterness and resentment toward my father. We reconnected, and he has been willing to talk about his decisions that affected me and take accountability for his mistakes during our conversations.

I respect and appreciate the fact that my father has been willing to revisit the past because all I wanted to gain was a better understanding so that I wouldn't pass these flaws on to my children. My father said he loved us but was too selfish during that time of his life and unwilling to deal with our mother, who was truly a woman of rage who always kept a gun and threatened to use it on everyone.

Once my father and I reconnected, I became eager to learn about him and his ways of thinking. I quickly realized that I thought the same way he did about some things, so I had to learn about him to ensure that I wouldn't repeat his mistakes. This was so important to me because my wife and children don't just mean something to me; they mean EVERYTHING to me. They are my reason for living and doing things the right way.

My father quit school after the eighth grade. Despite quitting school, he became a top insurance salesman, proving that he could achieve success despite his past—but he has been known for getting into challenging situations yet always finding a way to recover. I have also made risky financial decisions that set my family back numerous times, always feeling like I could make up for it—a pattern of my father's—however, I have always been committed, faithful, and determined to overcome all obstacles.

I do not want to pass on foolish thinking to my children. The conversations with my father exposed many of his poor decisions as well as my own blind spots, such as poor planning and emotional spending. My father helped me realize that I was duplicating some of his mistakes and helped me see the potential outcome of those bad decisions before they happened. The more transparent my father is with me, the more aware I become of the inherited habits. Though I should note that they are not all bad, because he did pass on the ability to sing.

The first thing my father tried to do with me after we reunited was to act like he could tell me what to do, as if he had been in my life the entire time. He often tried to do this with my sister and oldest brother; however, he found himself being addressed in a manner that he didn't like because they were not receptive to his method of communicating with them as adults. He would come by the house, wanting to take me to the store like I was a little kid and buy me something, but I was far beyond that stage of life.

I will say that you can recover, but it requires time, transparency, and trust-building to regain your voice. Those things can be painful because you must face the results of your decisions; however, God is able to help you overcome anything.

I let my father know that what I needed from him was not material things but the truth about the past and a willingness to share his life and discuss the decisions he made over the years. The purpose was to gain a better understanding of myself because I came from him, and I could possibly make some of the same decisions he did when facing some of life's situations.

Today, we have great conversations and a strong relationship; we talk almost every day. I am thankful for the time God allows us to have with each other despite it all. He did what he knew, and it's up to me to learn from his journey and make improvements in my own life.

I love my father despite his absence, and I knew that it was important for me to learn from both his mistakes and the good things he did to ensure that I always give my family the best of me. My commitment has been to prevent my children from experiencing the same harmful moments I did as a result of my father choosing to be selfish.

My father had some very good reasons for not being there, but at the end of the day, they were just excuses. Spread out over an eighteen-year period, I probably saw him for a total of eight months to a year. I say again, the reasons why my father left us are justifiable, but to a child, the best reason still sounds like an excuse at the end of the day.

My message to fathers is not to make excuses but to make a difference. Don't lose your voice with your family, because the life you save with this action may be your own.

If we abuse our children or their mothers emotionally

or physically, we are throwing away our own inheritance. We should be enjoying the lives of our children and our grandchildren, not trying to find a way to get back into their lives after exhausting ourselves with self-satisfaction. If we let it get to that point, we will likely be either replaced by someone else who cares enough to enjoy what we threw away or forced to accept the fact that someone else came on the scene and abused our families even further because we were not there to protect them. This is how children become angry and bitter toward their fathers.

For those of us with children, it is our duty to pour positivity and encouragement into their lives; doing that removes the ceiling of doubt and fear that could be hanging over them because of our actions. We must fight to prevent the distractions of this world from leading us to the destruction of our families. Thank you, God.

Fathers, make the choice to keep your voice by staying engaged and active in your children's lives; remember, the lives we save may be our own.

CHAPTER 4

Despised by My Mother, but God

Sometimes, people have children together, and then when the relationship between the parents ends in anger, they take out their frustrations on the innocent child or children. This can potentially become a repeated process of abandonment and abuse until someone breaks the cycle by choosing to be a better parent.

What I felt as a child was the anger of my mother toward my father; she talked badly about him all the time and expressed her frustration through verbal comments and physical contact. To top it off, I looked so much like my father that it made matters worse, especially during those moments of discipline that were filled with my mother's rage.

My mother, whom I loved and want to believe loved me in her own way, unfortunately, did not give the nurturing love that a mother gives in the form of a simple hug or saying, "I love you, and I am proud of you," with any consistency. Because she could not find fulfillment and happiness, she often stated how sick she was of having to deal with us and that she could not wait until we were out of her hair. Now, I am not making any excuses for my mother because she still made those decisions; I just have a better understanding of why things happened the way they did.

For example, my mother was aggressive and delivered words with anger and a hatred for being a parent so strong that you could feel it when she said them. Her attitude and vitriol had a lasting impact on me that has taken years to overcome. She was angry about life and treated her three children like it was our fault that she was unhappy. My mother hated my father because he left, she was angry about being responsible for us, and she didn't mind telling us that she should have flushed us down the toilet when she had the chance.

For years, I heard the echo of my mother's words in my ear: "You will never be nothing but a no-good bastard, just like your father." That statement would cause me to doubt myself at times. To overcome the echo in my ear, I had to hear positive words of encouragement from someone I considered credible, who saw potential in me and was willing to help me get beyond my internal challenges.

My mother never really got over my father, and she continuously expressed her anger toward him over the years. He hid himself from my mother by moving a lot, even going to jail once to prevent paying child support. This went on for many years, which made matters worse for my sister and me as children because we had the same mother and father, while my older brother had a different father who lived in New York.

My mother's anger toward my father made its way into his sister's (my aunt's) marriage, as my mother had an affair with her sister-in-law's husband, which ended their marriage. My aunt recently shared the story about how my mother's actions that caused her divorce. This is one of the reasons why my mother ended up leaving Virginia to live in New York City.

Sometimes, when I entered my mother's presence as a teenager, she would grit her teeth and say, "You make me sick to my stomach," as if she were looking at my father. I believe the burden of raising us frustrated my mother so much that she could not contain her anger and said things to us that you would expect to hear from an enemy in the street. In moments of discipline, it felt like she hated us with a passion and would have killed us if she could have gotten away with it.

The hatred wasn't just limited to me—I remember watching my mother choke my sister one day as if she were her ultimate enemy. My sister missed our family and friends in New York after we moved back to Virginia and had decided to make some long-distance phone calls to New York, which ran the phone bill up to about six hundred dollars. Our mother went off in rage toward my sister over that phone bill. At one point, I didn't think she was going to stop beating my sister. The altercation started out with lots of yelling and screaming but escalated quickly to blows to my sister's head and then choking her with both hands around her neck.

I saw the rage of my mother and the hurt of my sister at its peak at that moment, which is as clear to me today as it was during the actual event. My mother finally let go, and my sister eventually regained her ability to breathe normally again, but the impact of that experience led me to believe that my mother could hurt us really badly in a moment of rage or possibly kill one of us if she went too far.

The look on my sister's face was one of hurt, disbelief, and confusion because the violent experience came from our mother dealing with her like she was her worst enemy. We fought a lot in the projects of New York because that was a way of life, so we were accustomed to the violence outside. However, what we experienced in our own house was far worse than anything we ever dealt with outside of our home. I truly believe that God intervened in moments like that because His purpose for our lives has always been bigger than those painful moments.

As a teenager, I developed more than just a fearless mentality; I was willing to die for a season because I'd had enough, or so I thought. Not expecting to accomplish anything because my mother told me I wouldn't so often, I was at a point where I felt as though my life didn't matter. My mother had a gun that she was more than willing to use—she made many threats of blowing her own children's brains out. The story was that her father shot at his own family when he got drunk and abused his wife, so she was familiar with weapons and not afraid to use them.

My mother had a habit of slapping us in the face as an act of discipline. One night, when I was fifteen, I came into the house late. She proceeded to cuss me out, then drew her hand back to slap me in the face. I caught her hand and told her she would never slap me in the face again. I had reached my limit with enduring the physical abuse of my mother. She then told me that she would "blow my f***ing brains out," and in that moment, I stood there and said, "Do it." I really meant it; I was so sick and tired of dealing with my mother's rage. From that point, it was simply "whatever" for me, and my concerns about life for myself were fading away.

My mother never went after her gun, as I am sure she felt my sincerity in that moment. After realizing she wasn't going to get her gun, I simply turned around, went to my room, and closed my door. My mother didn't pursue me anymore that night, nor did she discuss it the next day. From that point, she still cussed and fussed at times, but she didn't try to get physical with me anymore.

Don't misunderstand me; I loved my mother. Despite her anger, she worked two jobs at times to put a roof over our heads, put some food on the table, and put some clothes on our backs. This is so important because realizing what she did and where she was coming from has helped identify the reason behind my mother's anger and the fact that she didn't quit in the fight. My mother's dream was shattered when my father left her to raise us by herself. Although she did her share of damage, I am still thankful for my mother's commitment to see me graduate from high school (even if she framed it as "You will graduate and get the f*** out of my house," she made a commitment because my Aunt Pearl told her that she had to see us through that part of our lives).

I was forced to learn how to become an adult on my own, which meant I thought I was ready for anything at fourteen or fifteen years old, but of course, I wasn't even close to being ready. I was left with a damaged view of how to interact with others and how to be a responsible young man because my father left me uncovered and unprotected.

The last two years of living in the house with my mother after my brother and sister moved on with their lives were tough. I had to endure her anger based on things they had done that I didn't deserve. I was not a perfect kid by any means, but I didn't put my mother through the things my siblings did. I think she was ready to get rid of me when they left, but I had two more years of high school, and she stuck it out until I graduated. I thank God for my mother's commitment.

It was obvious that she was extremely frustrated, though, as my mother would come home from work, enter the kitchen, and begin yelling and cursing about what she didn't like or something that wasn't done the way she wanted. Then she would go behind her bar and get a glass of Bacardi Rum and Coke, go upstairs to her room, slam the door, and yell some more about how sick of me she was and how bad she wanted me out of her house.

I still loved my mother and my father despite what I endured, and God's plan for my life has put me on a path of being married to the same woman and faithful to her for thirty-three years and counting. My immediate family and I have experienced a genuine love for one another that has become an example to many. Only God can create such an outcome.

As I've gotten older and gained distance from my

mother, I've gained some understanding of why things unfolded the way they did. Not to justify my mother's actions, but my mother and her siblings experienced a lot of violence in the form of alcohol abuse, physical abuse, emotional abuse, and more in their own families, and they passed that on to their children.

I found out that my mother was angry because she had wanted to be a stay-at-home mom. My brother also wanted to be the only child, and since I was the youngest, I had to deal with the anger he inherited from our mother. You can probably imagine some of the things my sister and I endured. Just about every action had to inflict some pain or cause tears to flow when our brother was involved.

For many years, my mother was angry because she was strapped with children and struggling financially, often wishing that she had total freedom to do whatever she wanted. From my point of view, she simply duplicated the anger that she experienced as a youth because she never got answers for her own internal struggles and refused to have a conversation about anything regarding her past.

My wife and mother-in-love experienced a taste of my mother's attitude and anger. Throughout the first twenty years of our marriage, my mother had not been to our house more than ten times despite many invitations. She would never show up to any of our children's events, just like she didn't show up for mine when I was growing up. I was accustomed to it, but my wife and my mother-in-love were not. After the first ten years, they began to understand that it wasn't just me when it came to my relationships with my mother and brother. They were confused about our distant relationships since I never said anything to them other than "If you only knew" for years because I was too guarded to say anything.

My wife and mother-in-love have enjoyed an incredible relationship as a family, totally the opposite of what I experienced, so my family stories would have been completely foreign and unimaginable to them, making it easy for me to keep them to myself.

My mother passed away December 17, 2020. We talked very little because she was still bitter and did not want to discuss things that had occurred in the past, which made it hard for me to find a way to have casual conversations with her. For me, having those conversations about our past was extremely important because there was a lot that she could have clarified for me that would have been helpful to my family. Despite it all, my wife and I reached out in an incredible way to help my mother, which you will read about later in the book. God is amazing.

The biggest thing I learned from my mother was the fact that she stayed the course to complete the assignment of seeing her three children graduate from high school. When she put me out of her house, it unlocked the drive in me to overcome adversity and keep going. I have been driven to prove her wrong by becoming the best I can be in all that I do. As I pause and reflect on the past, I am reminded of what I do not want to experience again in my life, so I work with a level of determination that ensures my family has a place they can call home and enjoy.

The greatest lessons I learned from my mother were to find a way to endure pain because it does not last, to overcome all obstacles relentlessly, to accomplish goals with good habits, and to sustain peace of mind by valuing people.

CHAPTER 5

Abused by My Older Brother, but God

To say I had a brother born for adversity is an understatement. Looking back, I truly believe my brother wanted to be an only child, and from my perspective, he was committed to driving a wedge between us every chance he got. Bullying me was fun to him, and he often laughed while I cried during so many moments. He was the obstacle course I was destined to overcome. As I reflect on my past now, I can finally see that this part of my journey was the training ground for me to become an adversity killer, capable of achieving what other people consider impossible.

My older brother and I have different fathers but the same mother. He was four years older and much bigger than I was for years while we were growing up, and he took full advantage of that until I would grab something to hit him with just to even things up. The fights became more frequent and more aggressive over the time I was nine to fourteen.

Now, I just want to say that despite it all, I still love my older brother; I just don't trust him.

For the first nine years of my life, I did what I thought was right by trying to love and follow my big brother, but that consisted of me being bullied and physically abused at times while I was awake and even sometimes while I was trying to sleep. He told me himself that he used to hit me while I was asleep, and I remember moments when I would wake up swinging my fist as if I were fighting someone. You see, this was fun for him. For those who think this is like your typical family interaction between siblings, think again. This dude used to hold me down by sitting on my stomach with his knees on my arms and would just hit me continuously until I cried for so long that I couldn't even make a sound anymore, and then he would just laugh about it.

Remember, my mother passed on her anger, and he wanted to be the only child. In fact, the only times he didn't come at my sister or me were when our older cousins stayed at our house because they would deal with him themselves. But when they left, he went right back to his usual self, and we caught hell again.

Even as I write this, it's like looking back and seeing someone else's story on television, even though I lived through it. Today, I can't imagine myself or my children being subjected to the things I had to endure.

On one occasion, when we lived in Bricktown, New York, my brother convinced my sister and me to run away. We did for about thirty minutes, but we turned back and came home because there was about two feet of snow on the ground we were trying to walk through, and we knew we wouldn't last long in that. Yeah, I know, I couldn't imagine my children doing something like that, but we were convinced that things shouldn't be like they were in our own home and determined to find something better.

There were times when we were at peace, but it didn't take much to turn nothing at all into a full-blown battle. My mother was unaware of a lot of the things that happened because she would be at work or would leave to go out on the town. Furthermore, my brother—who always controlled the situations—would convince me not to say anything regardless of what he was putting me through, so I wouldn't say anything unless there were visible bruises or cuts that had to be explained. I think if he had the guts, he would have taken me out and dumped me somewhere. Yeah, I know it seems crazy, but this is just a glance in the window of my life as a child.

We once got into a fight when I was nine, and I began

hitting him with all the strength I had in me, but of course, the fight ended with my head slamming into a glass door, putting a nice scar on my forehead as he slung me down a set of stairs. I realized trying to follow him would have cost me everything.

From nine years of age to fourteen, the fights got worse, and I was determined to get him back one day. Now, the source of my rage was rooted in a moment of molestation at the hands of my older brother that occurred at the age of nine. This unthinkable act was so damaging that I held the pain of this experience within me for more than thirty years. I could not bring myself to share this life-changing event with my mother, sister, or anyone else. I felt betrayed, violated, and guilty for allowing myself to be influenced by my brother's sadistic persuasion. In my mind, I wanted to erase the moment and act like it never happened, but the damage had been done, and I never looked at my brother in the same way as someone I could trust and follow. The action never happened again, but the impact lasted for many years. I became very guarded as a person and extremely protective of children, especially my own, against any perceived predators. As you read on, this moment will help clarify my relentless drive to become the best version of myself in all areas of my life as someone who has overcome adversity.

Now, as much as he fought with me, I remember one

time while we were living in New York when my brother let this guy punch him in the face twice and then ran. I saw this with my own eyes, which made me furious. You see, he was afraid of others out in the streets but was a bully to me inside the house, and of course, he was able to beat me up later that day, and I fought him even harder after seeing him run.

There were many fights between us during this period, and it became clear to me that separation was the only solution because he was not going to change, and my anger toward him continued to grow.

Here is a snapshot of one of our most dangerous episodes. When I was fourteen, we argued about something as we stood in the kitchen next to the sink. I must have unintentionally spit on him while we were yelling in each other's faces. I say that as an attempt to justify his next action because what he did in that moment was truly the act of your worst enemy. He grabbed my head with his hands on each side of my face, then gathered all the saliva in his mouth that he could and spit directly in my face. Of course, I lost it, and this started a fight between us that ended with my mother calling the cops from her job because we were home by ourselves and she could no longer handle the two of us in these moments of rage.

Before the police arrived, I had time to chase my brother around the yard with a butcher knife, but I was unable to catch him, so I left the house. I went down the street and grabbed my grandfather's shotgun from behind his bedroom door because we were within walking distance of my grandfather's house in Yorktown. I came back to the house and stood on the edge of the road with this big shotgun in my hands with about thirty yards between us. I pointed the gun at him as he stood in the doorway of our house, and believe it or not, he thought it was funny until I raised the gun up and pulled the trigger. Thank God there were no bullets in the gun. You see, the time it took for me to walk down to my grandfather's house was enough time for me to regain my thoughts and understand where I was, but in that moment, I still wanted to scare him. Thank you, God!

After standing there on the curb and pulling the trigger twice, he closed the door and moved away from it. It was enough for me at the time to see his reaction, so I walked back down to my grandfather's house to put the gun back. By the time I journeyed back to our house, a police officer and my mother had arrived in the driveway. I can only imagine what might have happened if the officer had arrived moments earlier while I still had the gun. Thank you, God.

I remember the police officer asking me questions, but I never responded to him. Since my mother was available to speak with the officer, she answered all his questions. I have no idea what she said to him, but it didn't really matter to me at that time since I was in an emotional state of mind.

During this fight, we also had an aunt who lived next door to us and had evidently yelled to get my attention while I was chasing my brother around the yard with the knife, but I had zoned out during that emotional moment and was unwilling to listen to anyone. I later apologized to my aunt for not responding to her when she yelled to get my attention. My sister, who was also in the house, didn't get involved because the fights were too extreme at this point.

This is real life for many families; a lot of the violence starts at home well before it ever reaches others outside of the home.

We got into one last fight after the worst episode, right before he left to go into the military. This time, our mother put herself between us, trying to stop us from killing each other or, more likely, stop me from killing him. I had finally gotten a good head shot in on him, but of course, it was after he had already punched me in the face. Nevertheless, I got one in, and we wrestled until we all fell on the bed. The fight only came to a halt then because our mother fell and we broke her glasses during the altercation. After hours had passed and the emotions had settled down, I knew we were truly a divided family, and I recognized that we couldn't be around each other without resorting to violence. My brother and I still stayed in the same room, but we said absolutely nothing to each other for the next two months, and I mean *nothing*.

He eventually graduated from high school and finally left the house to go into the military, and we didn't speak to each other much at all for about two years. During that period, he was discharged from the military and dropped out of college. He did send me a letter of apology, but I wasn't having it and was determined to get him back for all that he had put me through.

When he finally returned to my mother's house, I was in my last year of high school and ready for the fight of my life, or so I thought. You can't imagine how determined I was to get him back; I was full of bottled-up rage after enduring so many abusive moments at the hands of my older brother.

With every push-up, every squat, and every weight I lifted, I focused on getting him back. Now, I was just two inches shorter than him at six feet two inches and had become incredibly strong, relentlessly determined to win.

He came into our mother's townhouse; at the time, my mother and uncle were in the dining room, and I stood in the kitchen. We didn't say anything to each other; we simply crossed paths. Now, I don't know if I imagined it or not, but in my mind, he brushed my shoulder, and for me, it was time to win the war between us after losing so many battles. Within seconds, I had picked him up, taken him outside, and slammed him on the ground, daring him to move because I was ready to win this fight by any means necessary.

But after standing over him and seeing the hurt in his eyes, I couldn't go through with it. I was so...so angry because I couldn't do to him what he had done to me for years. I had convinced myself with all my bottled-up anger that it was payback time, and I was ready to end my frustration. I wanted to beat the breaks off of him, but I just couldn't understand why it bothered me so much to carry out my mission and give back to him what I thought he truly deserved.

So I left him lying there on the ground and went back into the house, where I met my mother and uncle at the door. They were trying to figure out what happened, but I said absolutely nothing and just went to my room and slammed the door.

Amazingly, people think you can just forget about those abusive physical and emotional moments that occur. Yeah, right! That's just a snapshot of things that occurred between my brother and me. You see, just writing this made me ball up my fist (just keeping it real). At times, I felt like I should have just worn his butt out anyway, but I may not have been able to stop, so I thank God for controlling my rage and providing, yet again, a way of escape.

It is so relieving to me that I can get this weight off me. Although I am in tears while typing these words, I can feel the shift in my mind. You see, I tried the method of just forgetting about it, but that turned into me having a hard external shell and being unwilling to trust anybody; at the first sign of someone looking or sounding like they were going to hurt me, I would assume the worst and respond accordingly by protecting myself or just walking away.

Today, I can say that my brother and I don't have a strained relationship because we don't have one at all. I think if he had shown remorse or any desire to be forgiven, it might have changed things, but he remains the same type of person even as an adult, or perhaps I just haven't been ready to receive any noise from him.

As of today, I have wanted to know what happened to him and better understand why he made some of those decisions. I can only imagine what went on in his mind. My prayers for his well-being are truly sincere now, and I say it that way because I have prayed for him in the past, but not like this, with sympathy and empathy for him. God is amazing.

This is the story of many, but most are unwilling to tell it because of shame or fear of ridicule, and I don't blame them at all. However, I have learned that the things we hold inside of us have a way of affecting our lives in some way or another in the long run. As for me, telling my story has produced mental healing and bonding in my immediate family because my wife and children have a much better understanding of why I am the way that I am, and this gives me a chance to improve.

These family discussions also gave me opportunities to apologize to my children for my errors as a father and to seek my wife's forgiveness for my mistakes as a husband. For at least the first fifteen years of our marriage, there was a part of me I would not allow my wife to access; even though she knew something was bothering me, she didn't know what it was.

As a result of my past with my brother, I never allowed my kids to be around him outside of my presence, and it wasn't often that I would be around him anyway. However, the bad part about this was that I didn't let my kids spend much time with my wife's brother either, which I regret because he loves the ground they walk on, and I know now that he would never have done anything to hurt them. Because I didn't share my childhood memories with anyone for so long, I was overprotective and aggressive around others for no apparent reason to them. No one knew about the things I endured at the hands of my older brother, nor were they aware of what was going on emotionally on the inside.

CHAPTER 6

The Benefit

What I gained from this adversity was an immeasurable amount of determination, the ability to endure pain, and a drive to overcome adversity. Any physical confrontation or competitive interaction became an opportunity to prove myself, and I often visualized myself competing against my older brother.

I realized that I never wanted to end up on the bottom, so within the first thirty seconds of a confrontation or competition, I would display a refuse-to-lose level of effort that would end a confrontation very quickly. The first thirty seconds of relentless effort was all about letting my opponent know just how hard I would be playing the entire game or fight.

As I look back over my career as an athlete, I cannot help but acknowledge the fact that all the adverse moments I endured at the hands of my older brother proved to be training grounds for me to learn to go beyond my wall of fatigue and pain. I would keep going until I reached the point of total exhaustion, then determine that quitting was not an option. I knew I could outlast my opponent if I just kept going as hard as I could. I played sports as if my life depended on it. The bigger my opponent, the harder I fought; I had no respect for size or strength because my experiences with my brother made me stoic when it came to physical contact.

Over my career as an athlete, I earned five MVP awards between football and basketball, I played arena football, I reached All-American status as a football player, I was inducted into the Mason-Dixon Semi-Pro Football League Hall of Fame in 2012, and I am now a 2019 Newport News Apprentice School Inaugural Hall of Fame Inductee and hold records in football, basketball, and track.

I became an adversity killer.

CHAPTER 7

A Sprinkle of Love

My sister and I share the same parents, so she was my sprinkle of love and protection whenever she could be during those challenging moments with our older brother. I will never forget the support of my sister, whether it was recovering from a battle with our brother or supporting me at one of my basketball games during high school.

I remember wearing second- and third-hand clothes for most of my childhood, until my junior year when my sister brought me a new outfit, the first one I had received while in high school. Before then, it was hard to imagine what it would feel like to wear something that fit me, something that I was wearing first. These were things that people around me took for granted. My sister picked me up and patched me up many times. Although she was the one who broke my two front teeth by slamming me on my face when I was eight years old, I think she cried more than I did. She loved me, and I knew it. We stuck together; even though we had our moments, I never felt like my sister wanted to really hurt me because she could have at any time, but we had your more typical brother-and-sister relationship—with a twist of violence, of course, because that's all we knew.

It was tough being the youngest while growing up in poverty because I would be favored by family members outside the house when we visited, but when we got home, I had hell to pay. I think it bothered my older brother more than anything.

Thankfully, we had an aunt who always stayed in our mother's ear and ensured we had something to eat and a place to stay. We'd visit Aunt Pearl from time to time, and she would always make sure we understood how to respect others. She made sure we respected our elders. She was more like our grandmother, and I fondly remember my aunt's love, hugs, and kisses. Although we didn't spend a lot of time around her, the moments we spent with her made a difference. I believe my aunt was the glue that kept us from destruction back then, as she would often give our mother words of wisdom and correction before giving her the money that she would ask for from time to time. We would also go to her house and get a good meal every now and then.

My mother left Virginia to live in New York when we were really young, and the first place we stayed was with our Aunt Pearl. I believe it was during that time that my aunt forced my mother to commit to seeing us graduate from high school no matter what; maybe she promised her something because when my aunt passed away, my mother inherited her house in Virginia.

I believe my aunt saw the pain we endured as children; she and my other aunt who lived in California (my Aunt Margarette) were both committed to helping my mother. Aunt Margarette once flew me out to Los Angeles to stay with her for two weeks, and it was as if I had escaped hell for a moment and saw a glimpse of heaven.

They were the best two weeks I had as a child. I didn't have to fight for food—there was plenty of it—I had my own room, my own bed, a new outfit, some shoes that fit, and my aunt gave me two dollars in quarters; you couldn't tell me I wasn't in heaven. She took me to Disneyland, which was so incredible, and I was exposed to a whole new world. I could even go outside and play with some kids who weren't trying to fight or destroy things.

My Aunt Margarette retired from the Air Force, and she lived in a totally different world than the rest of our family regarding being stable, settled, and free from the financial struggles of life. She was someone who gave me hope as a child.

My older cousins also treated me with love whenever we visited them or when they came to visit us. But for the most part, my sister was in the trenches with me, fighting through those tense moments of our childhood. On many occasions, my sister played the role of my mother; she provided those moments of genuine love and the push to be better, and she would tell me what my mother never did, which was, "I am so proud of you."

My sister still visited from time to time after she moved out of the house and away from our mother, always giving me something she wanted me to have because she knew we didn't have much. It wasn't just clothes but also food, like something as simple as a hamburger and fries. Although we had our battles, we recovered quickly like normal siblings would. And to this day, my sister is one of my biggest fans, no matter what I do. I love her to life, always.

CHAPTER 8

Making Sense of It All

As I put the pieces of this puzzle together, it makes a little more sense to me now, and I understand why I went through so many things as a youth and young man. My mother was raised in anger by an alcoholic father and wanted to be a stay-at-home mom, but after she had two more children with my father—who decided to leave her holding the bag with no support at all—after already having my older brother who wanted to be the only child himself, my mother was angrier than ever. What it looks like to me now is that she took her frustration with our father out on us, and since I looked just like him, she would often say that I made her sick and that I would be a no-good bastard just like him. Just craziness, but God had a plan all along.

My older brother wanted to be the only child, and seeing my mother strapped with two more children whom she appeared to be angry with all the time, from his perspective, gave him permission to act on her frustration toward us, and it was fair game to deal with us as he saw fit. What a journey!

Despite all the things I endured, God gave me a smile so strong that it contains my story within, along with the internal strength to overcome adversity. I am driven to seek the good in others and help them get beyond the pain of their pasts.

PART 2

The Family That Grew Me

*Me and "the man who stood in the gap,"
Coach Baggett.*

CHAPTER 9

The Man Who Stood in the Gap

After returning to Virginia when I was thirteen, I met Coach Doug Baggett, whom I think of as "The Man Who Stood in The Gap." Coach Baggett had the most positive impact on me, which has lasted more than thirty years and has changed my view of people in general. His actions have always been a reminder for me that there are some incredible people in this world committed to doing good things for others.

The violence between my older brother and me was spilling out of the house when I was thirteen to fifteen years old, the most critical time in life when young men determine their direction in life. The first day I met Coach Baggett was after getting into a fight with another student. He said, "I can get the boxing gloves for the two of you to finish this fight, or I can get the paddle and give each of you five licks."

Of course, I chose the boxing gloves, but the other kid said he was done and didn't want either option. The kid was a big bully who ran into an abused kid with nothing to lose. I think Coach Baggett saw that I had the potential to become a productive person in life and just needed some guidance. I wouldn't start any fights with anyone; however, I didn't back down from any either. I was still fighting at home with my older brother, who got fulfillment out of beating on me for reasons that only made sense to him.

During my freshman year at York High School, there was another situation with a bully that almost cost me everything. This kid was a senior football player who decided to take a football away from me and a group of my friends. Well, before I knew it, the situation got ugly; I had given him a chance to give the football back, but he decided to act big and bad in front of some cheerleaders who were close by at the time. My response was to go into a nearby trash can, find and break a glass bottle to create a jagged edge, and approach the football player. Of course, this action shocked everyone standing there, as I am sure they had never seen anything like that before. I had seen someone else do it while living in Baisley Projects, and the person who broke the bottle stabbed another person in the face with it. Thankfully, the football player decided to give the ball back. He ran his mouth while standing behind a cheerleader, but thank God it ended there with no further actions. You see, I needed some guidance before I did something that would have cost me everything. Thank you, God.

It turns out that Coach Baggett was the baseball and basketball coach at York High School, and he could flat-out shoot a basketball better than anyone I had ever seen. Eventually, I became a very productive athlete, but before that ever happened, Coach Baggett reached out to me as he did with many others—whether they were athletes or not—and put quality time in with me as a coach and mentor. Coach welcomed me into his home, took me fishing, taught me how to catch soft shell crabs, and would take me out every now and then to get a hamburger from Pop's Restaurant.

Coach showed me unconditional love, wanting absolutely nothing in return other than to see me become the best I could be in life. He became my way of escaping the chaos I was dealing with at home and showed me that there was so much more to life than the violence and abuse I experienced there.

Coach Baggett accepted me as I was; he never talked down to me, nor would he let anyone else either. I remember one day when another coach said something sideways and Coach Baggett jumped on him immediately, making it very clear to the other coach that his inappropriate comments would not be tolerated. He allowed me to stay in his home because I believe he knew I was safer there, and my mother didn't care where I was during that time anyway.

You see, anything could have happened to me during that time of my life, but I know without a shadow of a doubt that Coach Baggett was divinely assigned to cover me as a father, coach, and mentor. Thank you, God.

I will never forget Coach Baggett and what he did for me in such a trying season of my life. Coach Baggett has been a father to me for the rest of my life, and I am forever grateful to him. He still refuses to let me give him anything in return, so I take advantage of every moment to pay it forward to someone else. There are many kids today who have similar struggles and simply need someone to believe in them.

I made it through the ninth grade by making my way onto the basketball team. I was the last player to make the team, but by the time I was a sophomore, I had become the leading scorer. I played like my life depended on it, non-stop and relentlessly from one end of the basketball court to the other. The opportunity meant everything to me, and the fact that I could put on a uniform that belonged to me was incredible.

During my sophomore year in high school, I stayed with five different friends just to make it through the school year because my mother had relocated again to a neighboring city, and I wanted to stay where I was, close to Coach Baggett and my team. It made a huge difference for me to have someone I could trust, and I didn't want to lose that.

I was one of those kids who never asked for anything. I could be hungry but wouldn't ask for food because I was too embarrassed and refused to be a burden on anyone. However, when I did get a chance to eat, the food was gone in less than five minutes.

Coach Baggett and some of my teammates' parents often had to tell me that it was okay, they had plenty of food. I would consume food so fast that they thought I was just swallowing it and not chewing the food at all. That same year, I slept on floors, couches, and sometimes a bed to make it through that season. I often wore the same clothes because all I had were three pairs of pants and four t-shirts that year, but I was extremely thankful for the help I was given during that humbling time in my life.

Academically, I failed English my sophomore year and had to go to summer school, but I made it through by the grace of God. When I look back on that scenario, it's hard to believe I didn't fail more classes.

I eventually transferred to Denbigh High School because that was the school zone my mother moved into, and my journey as a driven athlete continued.

CHAPTER 10

A Coach's Impact

I met two additional mentoring coaches at Denbigh High School: Ben Moore and Dennis Koutoufas, who took the time to invest and impart words of wisdom into my life.

Against the odds, I became one of the best athletes in the area and was in the newspaper. I led Denbigh High School to the first Christmas Tournament Championship and earned the tournament MVP award, the first Peninsula District Title, and the District Tournament Title as the leading scorer and rebounder. But through all this, I was unsupported by my mother, who didn't see me play much at all. I would bring home trophies and news articles, but she never came to the games. In fact, for my senior game in high school, I was escorted onto the basketball court by Coach K's wife so I wouldn't be alone when my fellow senior teammates had their parents with them. I think I just felt empty that whole night; no matter how hard I tried to ignore my feelings and just play, I couldn't get over that empty feeling I had on the inside.

People wondered why I played basketball so hard, but they didn't know it was my lifeline back then and my reason for believing in anything or anyone for that matter.

I thank God for the time Coach Ben Moore spent helping me polish my game in the gym and the time Coach K spent feeding, leading, and embracing me along the way. I was the coaches' toughest athlete at that time and kept the other players in line as an enforcer of the rules that the coaches put in place. I played like basketball meant everything to me and wouldn't allow my teammates to play with anything less than their best effort. This helped us win games most people thought we would lose because we were an undersized team. We defied the odds because other teams didn't play as hard as we did, and we played like our lives depended on overcoming the odds of winning games that appeared to be impossible.

CHAPTER 11

Growing Despite Thorns and Weeds

Even though I had success on the basketball court, I still experienced my mother's rage at home because she simply wanted me out of her house. This led to the most impactful moment between me and my mother. One day, she told me that I had to leave or she would call the cops and have them put me out. I had recently graduated from high school and was in the Newport News Apprentice School, so she had fulfilled her responsibility of getting her children through high school.

Though I was still hoping for a better relationship despite all the abuse and anger, unfortunately, I had to move on and leave without experiencing the nurturing love of my mother. Before that final moment, when I got into the Newport News Apprentice School, my mother told me that my paycheck was hers and that I had better give her the money or get out of her house. Now, I was more than willing to give her money, but not my entire paycheck. I had no problem with learning a lesson about being responsible, but I did have a problem with how she was trying to teach me that lesson.

At that time, I did what I thought were the right things, so I didn't feel like I deserved the frustration from my mother at this stage. I refused to give her my entire check, and that eventually led to me being put out of her house for good. I vowed never to live with my mother again, even if that meant sleeping in a car or worse. I found out years later that my sister had felt the same way; she had found temporary residence for her children and slept in her car just so she wouldn't have to be in the house with our mother, which let me know that I was not alone in my thinking.

To some people, it may be a normal or typical story, and it might seem like the right thing to do to someone, but for me, it felt like my last lifeline had been severed. I truly hoped to see the loving mother I dreamed of having show up in her, but that dream ended that day she had me put out. I loved my mother anyway, and I wanted to do things to make her happy after getting into the apprentice school. Even though I had other opportunities to go to college, I took advantage of the chance to make money and still play basketball with the hope of putting a smile on my mother's face, but in the end, she simply wanted me out of her house.

When she put me out, I was beyond hurt and determined to make it; I committed to becoming self-sufficient, no longer returning to my mother's house for shelter ever again. I felt like the only person left for me to trust and rely on was myself. Even though God had sent some people my way who took the time to share some words of encouragement with me, I struggled to get past the fact that I yearned for the mother's love and father's guidance that was never present during that critical time in my life.

Inside me, it felt like a piece of my heart was removed, and I never looked at my mother the same way after that. That moment became a time of reflection on all the things I had experienced, and I realized that she wasn't just angry when she said all of those ugly things. I believe she meant every word filled with anger and hate she ever said, wishing that she really did flush me down the toilet when she had the chance.

I do appreciate the fact that my mother provided a roof over my head and something to eat, so I thank her for that. You see, sometimes all we need to do is show up and be a positive presence in our children's lives, and their whole world changes for the better—that's if we bring the right attitude and commitment to love them as their parents.

CHAPTER 12

The Reminder

Many years ago, when my youngest children were nine and eleven, they wanted to walk next door to see my older brother, who lived beside our mother. Of course, they had no idea what had happened between us because I never talked about my past to anyone. So, I let them go, but right after they left, I immediately followed them just to make sure they would be all right.

I was not prepared for that visit, and my emotions got the best of me. My son and daughter sat on one couch with another young man while I sat opposite them, next to my niece and her mother. When my brother came out of his bedroom, all the things of my past that I was holding inside of me hit me at once. With my children watching, I, their father, someone they had viewed as a hardcore, rugged man, burst into tears like a child and was only able to say to my older brother, "I wanted to kill you." He made some smart remark in response. At that time, one of our cousins walked into the house. Witnessing emotions that he'd never seen from me before, it became clear to him why I stayed away from my brother.

All I could think about at the time was getting my children out of there. My children got up and said goodbye while I fought back the urge to react with my emotions, working as hard as I could to regain my composure. By the grace of God, we made it out of the door with no issues. Even though my brother knew he couldn't handle me physically at this stage, he still tried to be aggressive by bumping me with his elbow when I gave him dap as we were leaving. God intervened and made a way to escape.

After I stepped outside, I had an eye-opening conversation with our cousin, who was unaware of our past encounters and was completely stunned by what he learned in that moment. I shared with him that my brother was often abusive toward me as a youth; when we'd visit them from time to time and our cousin would rough up my brother, it was giving my brother a small dose of his own medicine. My cousin now understood that those moments when my brother received the punches meant everything to me.

For more than thirty years, I said nothing to other family members about our internal family struggles, so they only heard what my mother and brother said about why I was so distant from them. My cousin also shared the story about our grandfather getting drunk from time to time and shooting at our parents when they were children, and they would crawl under the house or stay in the woods until our grandfather fell asleep.

My brother's reaction to our cousin walking in on the situation was to cut off all communication with him. My brother had no idea what I shared, but he knew his one-sided story was shattered. My sister said she would defend me in those conversations with our family members, but they would just say that she and I were both crazy. We would hear those famous words, "But they're your family." Now, my sister did not hold the pain within her like I did because she would let them have it, as they say, "for free." I didn't have her strength to hold back the physical part because it was all or nothing for me, so I just stayed away.

My brother continued his abuse with his own family, which he managed to break up. My sister concluded that he is still the same, just older, so "don't waste your time trying to see if it's you because it's always been him." I needed to hear that because, as a man of God, I have prayed and fasted for understanding, forgiveness, and peace.

I would even force myself to take my family to see my mother when they were younger, but I would quickly leave if my mother even raised her voice one octave or reminded me of those moments in the past. I would leave regardless of what we were doing at that time.

My mother was full of anger and would verbally go off, but she learned quickly that I no longer had any tolerance for that. There were times when we'd be at the table eating something and my mother would go back to that place of anger, and I would immediately stop everything, even if I had just put a fork full of food in my mouth. I would pack up and leave with no regret because I refused to subject my family to that or myself to that ever again.

My older brother went to jail for a short period of time due to a domestic issue trying to protect his daughter, and I decided that I would go and have a conversation with him alone for the first time in years. All he heard for the next twenty minutes was me revisiting the fact that I wanted to kill him. I don't remember all that I said in that moment, but it was all related to me dealing with the hurt I experienced at his hands and the fact that he had no remorse for his actions. You see, I kept it all inside me, talking to no one about my past until then. I didn't get much out of him in that conversation, but it was a moment of relief for me. To this day, he hasn't changed much—even at the age of fifty, he still tried to pick a fight with our sister over something foolish.

I thank God every day for His grace and mercy because things could have turned out so differently.

CHAPTER 13

Still Destined

I faced a situation at nineteen years of age where a friend of mine was having an altercation with someone and another individual approached him with a gun and threatened to shoot him. The willingness to die I'd experienced when I was fifteen after years of my mother's emotional abuse showed its ugly head again; without hesitation or a second thought, I found myself in the face of the guy with the gun in his hand, pointed my finger in his face and pounded my chest, and told him that if he was going to shoot somebody then shoot me. My God, my God.

The guy could have shot me in reaction to my aggression. I was out of control, and as I look back at that situation, I now realize that God was protecting me from myself. The young man put his gun away, turned around, and went back to his apartment, where a group of his friends were on standby. Then I snatched my friend up and sent him on his way, and he jumped in his car and left.

There I was, standing up against five guys, challenging them instead of waiting for them to challenge me. I was out of control and had no regard for the threat I faced, but like I said, God was protecting me from myself. Amazingly, nothing other than an exchange of words happened, and I eventually walked back to my apartment. Thank you, God, for your intervention.

After that occurrence, the internal message to me was that I could either choose to change my ways or die young. My firstborn child was a year old, and I didn't want to abandon her like my father did with me, but I had no idea how to be a father.

During this time, the mother of my oldest daughter and I were just too immature to be parents as a couple. We were not committed to one another, which created problems that eventually ended our relationship. I eventually moved into my own place with two roommates, one who looked up to me and my craziness at the time as a role model and one who was a fellow basketball player. We would all hang out together back then, but I knew that it was time for a change since I was a new father. Some of my decisions at that time were selfish and inconsiderate. I got into altercations at times with others and even started carrying a gun myself, which was a bad idea for me, considering the violence I had experienced my whole life.

Even with a child, I was having thoughts of dying early, so I needed to make a change. I truly believe that God was pulling at my heart because around the same time, a lady at work came around my job and witnessed to me about God. She wasn't overbearing or overly aggressive; she was simply planting another seed of goodness in my life. As I look back, it is without a doubt that she was a heaven-sent angel.

Amazingly, not long after that, I met the woman who would eventually become my wife, and we started going to a church that turned out to be the same place the lady who planted the seed of goodness was a faithful member of. It was obvious to me that the power of God was at work because the virtuous woman who became my wife filled an incredible gap in my life. She made me feel like I had something important to accomplish, and she was willing to help me achieve it. My roommates immediately knew something was different about me because my actions changed almost instantaneously.

Unfortunately, not long after I had surrendered my life to God, I lost one of my roommates. He was shot and killed after moving back to New York. The other roommate had someone pull a gun on him and broke his jaw with the gun instead of shooting him. I've always thought that if I had been with him the night the guy pulled the gun on him, I might have lost my life by killing the guy or getting killed. I was devastated by the fact that I had been such a poor example of a leader to my roommate who was killed and such a bad influence on the other one.

I know I didn't force them to make any decisions, but my example of being a so-called tough guy impacted them. So, I vowed never to be a bad example to anyone else for as long as I live. It has been my way of doing right by the roommate who lost his life since I can't go back in time and change the way that I lived as an example to him.

It felt like God sent a rescue team to counter my way of thinking at that time because my soon-to-be wife and her mother loved not only me to life but also my daughter as if she were theirs. God was doing quick work in me, and I was faced with choosing to live a better life or not living all, so I accepted the salvation of Christ and committed to serving God at the age of twenty-one. God began renewing my mind from that point on, and I have served Him ever since.

CHAPTER 14

The Loaded Question

"If your mother or brother were to pass away, would you cry at their funeral?" This question asked by a friend initiated my journey of healing from within. My response was, "I don't know, but if I had to give a quick answer, it would be 'No,'" and he said, "There is no way you can be the man of God you are and not have a relationship with your family."

The only thing I would say to him and others was, "If you only knew," because I wasn't ready to share anything about the accounts of my past at that time. But I knew I had to make those uneasy phone calls of forgiveness to my mother and brother if I was ever going to experience healing from within. Several years before this moment, I tried to talk about what I experienced as a child with my wife and children, but I lost control of my emotions, so I stopped talking about it. I had shed so many tears as a youngster that I vowed not to cry anymore because my tears didn't help me as a child, and I had no intentions of crying about anything as an adult. I would literally hold my breath to prevent shedding tears, not realizing that it was the very thing I needed to do.

I explained my past to my wife by saying that we just didn't have a relationship like her family, but all I would hear was, "That is your mother and your brother," then I would respond by saying, "You just don't understand."

I have learned that reaching the act of forgiveness doesn't come easily, but it is so necessary. As we have been forgiven of our own shortcomings, we must learn to forgive others.

It took someone asking me that loaded question that forced me to deal with my emotions for me to realize I needed closure in that area of my life. My coworker and I routinely talked about loving our families, but I always referred to my wife and children rather than my parents and siblings because we just didn't have that type of relationship.

I can only conclude that God led him to ask me that loaded question because it was filled with mirrors that began exposing areas in me that needed healing. God has a way of getting us on the right track by using people to share the wisdom we need at the right time, no matter where we are in our lives.

I finally broke the ice and began sharing my story with my wife. It took EVERYTHING in me to build up enough strength to open my mouth and begin taking this emotion-filled journey in conversation because I had been trying to portray this superhero of a man hardened by his past.

I realized that my wife had simply been waiting on me; she always knew there was something that bothered me, and she also knew that this would be no everyday conversation. My wife confirmed that she has my back and is a protector of my heart. As I shared some of those moments with her, the tears began to roll down my face in a way that I could no longer control. She made me feel safe even though I felt broken on the inside. At the end of this extremely emotional conversation, my wife said, "Honey, you need to start writing it down in a journal." That conversation with my wife started a chain reaction that inspired me to begin sharing some of my childhood experiences with others, and the healing process began.

Over the next few years, I experienced an unexplainable feeling of freedom from the judgment of people. Now, I am driven to tell my story after hearing some of the testimonies of younger and older folks who have experienced similar painful moments but were initially too afraid to share them with anyone.

Even though it was more than thirty years since I had lived with my mother, for the first time, I could address some of the hurt in a conversation with my mother, and I brought back to her remembrance some of the things that occurred. She didn't recall a lot of it because she was under the influence of alcohol, or she just chose not to remember any of it.

I have now shared parts of my past with others several times, and each time, I get this unexplainable feeling of relief that overtakes me. I have to stop talking sometimes because my emotions get the best of me. It feels like a huge boulder has been lifted off my back. My mind is lighter, and I guess that is a form of stress relief. I am more confident in several areas of my life, which are all connected to leadership and the will of God. It has been an incredible experience of relief that has allowed me to be in a better position to help my family and others.

Dealing with my scars has been the most effective thing I have done for my family. I'm not making excuses or justifying my bad habits but simply creating awareness of my flaws and accepting responsibility for what I have done to myself and my family by not allowing myself to heal from within. Digging into the past hurt, learning from it, and sharing the lessons with others has made me a better husband, father, grandfather, mentor, coach, leader, and worshipper of the God who has kept me sound-minded all these years.

I have learned that help is available all around us, but when we're closed off or isolated, we sometimes reject the help we need to reach our full potential in life.

I wrote a song that played on a local radio station some years back, and someone called me on the phone after hearing the song and interview that I had on the radio. The young man told me that he was headed down the path of committing suicide, but hearing the song gave him hope, and he ultimately changed his mind to live and not die. I was stunned, wondering how he got my phone number, and I was thankful he chose to live. Even though I hadn't shared any of the moments of my past on the radio during that interview, I'm assuming that he could sense the deliverance in the tone of my voice.

Now, I realize that I am not alone; there are many folks who have suffered through similar things, from young adults to the elderly. Many folks tell me their stories in confidence and often confirm the fact that it was helpful to hear someone else share their story, as it gives them the courage to tell their own and experience personal healing.

Sharing my story reminds me of being in a classroom full of students when the teacher lectures on something that at least half the class doesn't understand, but no one is willing to raise their hand to say it. No one wants to feel embarrassed by not knowing the answer, but that one person in the room who says, "I'm not leaving without understanding the lesson" will ask the question, and everyone benefits from the answer. Someone has to step out and be courageous enough to share their own story so others may benefit from it.

I feel so much better after telling my story because it's like going to therapy, except I don't have to enter an agreement with a therapist—not that there's anything wrong with that form of healing because that works for many folks. A word of caution, though: you must be free from the judgment of people when you tell your story to someone who isn't legally obligated to keep your story confidential, because the people you tell may share your story with someone else.

I thank God for leading Brian Baker to ask me that loaded question.

CHAPTER 15

Moving On

At the beginning of our marriage, my wife and I would participate in things with my mother and older brother because I tried to ignore my internal reality and my wife had no idea about what I was dealing with on the inside. You see, those moments for me were like trying to ignore a pain that felt as if it was swelling on the inside. For the most part, I didn't say very much at all in those moments because I thought I would explode with emotion. But when we had our children, I became fearful of putting my children in the presence of my mother and brother because of what I had experienced with them. Knowing that they hadn't really changed much at all, I chose to protect my children by keeping them away from my mother and older brother.

I definitely didn't want my brother to even hold my children; just keeping it real. I knew that if either of them did anything to my children, it would have compromised the stability of my immediate family because I would have responded in a protective manner. I only allowed my children to be in their presence when I was there to observe *EVERYTHING*. I would have gone off on my mother or brother, and my wife would have been clueless as to why I went there, so I felt I had to protect her from seeing an uncontrollable measure of rage come out of me in response to them.

It is truly amazing that some people can't imagine going through the things that others go through—that's why it's easy for others to say, "Just forgive and forget"—but when you've lived through challenging and unforgettable moments that impacted your life, it takes time to overcome them. It's a journey of its own, and you must decide if you're willing to endure the pain while seeking release from the past. Whenever I have deep conversations with others about things like this, I always point the person back to seeking the answer that comes from within them because that's where the answers reside, but it takes someone building trust and then asking the right questions to reach those answers that come from within.

All I am saying is that for me, I had to confront my

issues by talking about them and finally relieving myself of the stronghold that had shackled my mind to things that occurred in my past. My relief didn't come through attending sessions with a counselor—although that process will work for many. For me, sharing my story with my wife allowed me to break through that initial barrier of emotions, and it was like going back in time and revisiting those hurtful moments all over again.

After that initial experience of releasing my story, I began sharing my journey with others. I believe God sent the right people my way, and the transparent conversations I've had have created moments of deliverance for me and others. To date, the biggest moments of relief came after I followed my wife's recommendation to begin writing a journal, which has now turned into this book. God is so amazing!

CHAPTER 16

Appreciation for Where I'm From

I am forever grateful for the coaches and parents who took the time to share words of encouragement, food, and sometimes shelter with me during such a critical time in my life. It is without a doubt that the hand of God was at the wheel because there would always be some unexpected person who would show up just in the nick of time to save me from self-destruction. This kept me moving forward in life on the path of becoming a productive person in society and a positive influence on others around me.

Now married for more than thirty-three years, my wife and I have taken it upon ourselves to be providers for many children over the years, even some who were less deserving than others because some kids had no desire to do right. As I go back and visit Coach Baggett from time to time, we often talk about helping others, and he once advised me to be careful because you can't save every kid, and some will misuse your kindness. He was correct because we had a few kids committed to doing just that.

I am truly amazed because I can see my story playing out in others without them saying anything. I identify it by how guarded and defensive they are at times in their emotional moments and interactions with others.

Today, as I reach out to mentor other young men who have faced similar struggles in their lives, I've been able to show them love, which is the entry point to reaching someone who thinks like I did, as well as show them respect because they are fearless. I will warn you, though, don't confuse showing these young men respect with showing them fear because if you show fear, they won't respect you.

After getting their attention, I give them the support they need to believe in themselves, which has put several of them in a position to become good fathers and good husbands. I am just so amazed at how God has brought me through so many challenging moments and has established me as a productive husband, father, and mentor in the community.

I am much wiser now, thanks to God's grace, and I lay

my life down every day for my family as a husband and father. My wife and children give me more than love; they give me a reason to live. I have also been given the determination to stay committed to my wife and the passion to keep my voice with my children. I am so thankful for the little things, appreciating life every day and taking advantage of the opportunity to make a difference in the lives of others. I have learned that if we really want to see things change, we must do something to create it.

After all of this, I now realize that God has been preparing me for His plan the entire time. I have been preparing to cross a bridge in my life, and on the other side of the bridge is my purpose and promise from God to live a fulfilled life of love for mankind.

From my view, it is without question that the grace and mercy of God will sustain us as we encounter the challenges of life, and the key is to accept the help He sends our way.

PART 3

The Family That Loves Me

Coach Baggett, who I met as a young teenager, and my mother-in-love, who I met at 21, were in attendance to see the results of their love shared with me as I was inducted into the inaugural Newport News Apprentice School Hall of Fame (bottom left). Along with my wife of more than 33 years, Kimberly, they are bookends for me on my pathway to becoming the best version of myself.

CHAPTER 17

Appreciating My Wife

My wife and I first crossed paths at a time in our lives when we weren't really interested in meeting anyone because we were both dealing with similar relationship challenges, so we exchanged phone numbers but didn't talk to or see one another over the next two years. Then, one night at an end-of-the-year Christmas party, we crossed paths again, and it was like the stars just lined up perfectly. We were basically inseparable after that moment—even though we were in denial about the connection between us.

That night, we had both come out just to have a good time, but we ended up talking for about four hours after leaving the party. It was as if all the things we had experienced had prepared us for one another, starting that night. The two years between our first two meetings allowed us to rid ourselves of all that we no longer wanted to deal with in a relationship, and we were able to start climbing the mountain of building a relationship that inspires others.

The young lady I met was strong and confident with a warm, outgoing personality that made her extremely attractive from the inside out. She has always been a beautiful woman; however, her beauty from within far exceeds what people see externally. With her heart and soul, she has expressed and displayed her support for my dreams and desires. She is my perfect fit!

We were born on the same day and even in the same hospital, but we grew up in two totally different environments. We are very similar in how we think and have equal respect for marriage. We committed to be in a relationship with each other in August of 1990 and were married in April of 1991. This woman has made me feel so complete from the very first hug; it's like we became the perfect match for each other. Now, that doesn't mean we have a perfect relationship, but we are very protective of each other. We do have our moments; however, what's big to us may be extremely small to others. She has proven to be everything I need in a woman, and there is nothing I wouldn't do for my wife.

Our laughter is fulfilling. What I mean by that is after more than thirty-three years of marriage, we can still make each other laugh uncontrollably.

My wife is very mature and was more than ready for the responsibility that came along with being a family. She made sacrifices early and often in our marriage while I was still growing up; this lasted for the first five to seven years of our marriage.

She paid the bills, managed our paperwork, did the shopping when we had the money to do so, and did whatever it took to ensure our family was on the right track. I had a two-year-old daughter at the time, and she loved her as if she had given birth to my daughter herself. In fact, during that challenging journey of raising my oldest daughter, my wife became the one she gravitated toward because of my wife's unwavering, unconditional love.

She has always made me feel like I am her king, whether we are in public or at home. It's amazing because we love on each other in public the same way we do at home. We both have zero tolerance for foolishness when it comes to infidelity or betrayal, and my wife has always been willing to sacrifice everything to make me happy.

My wife has supported me in everything I have done, even when she had to come behind me and clean up a mess that I may have made.

I think for the first few years of our marriage, she played a parent's role for me from time to time, especially after we had our son, as I was learning how to be a good husband and to be the best father I could without having an example to follow.

She always made sure I was taken care of and our children were provided for. She would work extra hours to add more funds to our bank account while I learned how to be unselfish and more sacrificial to ensure our family was taken care of first. She is my number one fan, and she makes me feel like I am what matters to her the most. If I could make her every dream come true, I would do it in a heartbeat. I love my wife, and I know that she loves me; knowing she has my back frees me to become the best that I can be.

CHAPTER 18

Putting Her First

After all these years, I have finally learned to put my wife first, as she has always put me first, even though I thought I was already doing that. You see, just because I brought home my paycheck and spent most of my time at home or around my family, I still found a way to make my wife feel secondary with my words and actions. For example, my priorities became apparent by looking at our conversations: I always talked about whatever was on my mind first.

I realize now that putting my wife first starts with me listening to her intently and allowing her to discuss what's important to her and how she feels about things. Then, after addressing or responding to those things that matter to her the most, I can begin talking about what's on my mind. It has taken me until now to realize that she has loved me with her ears by listening to my heart. Learning to listen to my wife earlier in our marriage would have decreased the number of errors I made along the way. Thank God for grace!

CHAPTER 19

My Pet Peeve

One of the things I had to do early in our marriage was eat my food while it was hot. When our children were between one and four years old, I was so selfish that my wife would wrestle with the kids while I enjoyed my food because I was determined to eat first. Although she didn't mind doing that because she didn't have to eat her food while it was steaming hot, I could not see the impact it had on her because I was focused on myself.

My wife has a heart of gold and never complained, but I didn't realize how it felt until we went out to eat one day with our grandson and I wrestled with him while my wife ate her food. There was my plate of food, hot and ready to be consumed, and my wife said to me, "Honey, you handle it this time." You would think after her many years of sacrifice that this would be a no-brainer for me, but keeping it real, initially, I was hot on the inside. However, I quickly got the point because my wife was more than deserving and our grandson was in need. As far as my meal, I quickly realized what was more important, and I didn't even eat the meal because I spent that time feeding our grandson. Since I had initially gotten upset, I chose to take my food home and give it to our nephew, who is always hungry, and he enjoyed every bite.

Even though my wife knew I needed to endure this moment and not pass our grandson over to her because I was determined to grow, she couldn't enjoy her meal to the fullest, knowing I was struggling. I know that my wife would lay her life down for me, as she has already done by having our children and in so many other ways.

CHAPTER 20

Not My Car

That was just one example of my wife sacrificing herself for our family, so here is another: I always had to enjoy whatever new car we had first. As time went on, we were able to afford two cars.

I had the car of my dreams—that my wife approved of me purchasing—but after driving it for a year, she told me that I put the car before her and our children. Of course I said, "No way!" However, it wasn't about my perspective; my family's view mattered the most, and my children confirmed my wife's observation. By the way, notice that I said my car, which did everything a car could do and had all the available features a car could have, but at the end of the day, it was just a tin can on wheels.

So here I was, facing a situation where I would either make a selfish or unselfish decision, and no matter how hard I tried to explain to them that I was just trying to make the car last by taking care of it, they were not buying it. While that was my truth, it wasn't reality based on their perception.

I decided to take this opportunity to show my family how much I love them by getting rid of something that I really wanted. I couldn't believe they thought that I valued a material possession more than my family.

Now, someone told me that the thought of trading my car in was a noble act, but what they didn't understand was how much my family means to me. Even though it might seem unthinkable from a man's perspective and numerically made no sense at the time, it was one of the best decisions I ever made.

After my children confirmed my wife's perception, I made my way to the dealership without hesitation, and when it was all said and done, the car was gone, my wife had a brand-new vehicle, and my kids were amazed at the fact that I had gotten rid of the car. I only drove my wife's brand-new car if we went somewhere as a family. This proved to be tougher than I thought, but I couldn't have done anything more right as a father and husband who wants to be the best example I can be to my children and others.

CHAPTER 21

Meeting Her Needs

Giving up my car proved to be the beginning of several sacrificial actions to show my wife how much I love her and how much she means to me. This action laid the foundation of support that my wife needed in order to endure six surgical procedures and more than a month in the hospital. I have learned to appreciate my wife so much more, and I am committed to showing her in ways that make her feel appreciated. Not according to how I think, because I might think that I am showing her appreciation by washing the car and putting gas in it for her, and while that is good, it's what is most important to her that really matters to me. To my wife, appreciation is relieving her of some of the things she takes care of on a routine basis. For instance, cleaning the entire house and taking care of the clothes every now and then, while setting her up to just go somewhere of her desire. In the end, it's a win for both of us because we get to experience peace of mind.

My wife means everything to me, and she has literally been the air I breathe. I remember hyperventilating in the emergency room one day. When the nurse ran to get me a bag, I asked my wife to come stand beside me, I wrapped my arms around her, and I was breathing normally again within seconds. This was amazing to the nurse because it wasn't normal.

My wife worked so hard for many years while I was still growing into manhood and the responsibilities that came with it. Being faithful to her has always been the easy part, but there were other areas I needed to grow in, and she has always been a rock during my immature state of mind. Bringing her home from work at a young age for a season was the least I could do, and my prayer now is to help her enjoy life to the fullest while appreciating her every step of the way.

CHAPTER 22

The Storm

This part of our journey begins with clarifying the fact that my wife had been a homemaker for several years, and while she may tell you that it wasn't the greatest financial decision because of the financial limitations, it did have its benefits. Before the storm hit us, I worked plenty of overtime at my job and made more than we did when we had two incomes. It appeared that we had no financial worries because we were doing things that we were unable to do in the past. However, we didn't save enough money for the rainy day others warned us about.

We were on a financial high for about six straight years, not expecting anything to go wrong, but low and behold, it did. The storm started out like a cloud that began to linger above us, but it quickly turned into the worst financial storm we had ever seen.

My wife had been dealing with physical discomfort for a long time and reached a point in 2011 where she began to express real concern. So, I told her that she needed to get something done because her health was a top priority. Well, the doctor's visit turned into my wife having a surgical procedure.

Prior to this, our son had just come through a surgical procedure himself and was headed to college on a basketball scholarship. As soon as we had come through his recovery and paid off the doctors' bills that were not covered by my insurance, we had to deal with the expenses that came along with sending a child to college. The small reserve we had was now gone.

While we worked on addressing my wife's physical discomfort, I also went through a season at my job where I worked less overtime due to a change in my area of responsibility. This meant I wasn't bringing home the same amount of money that had made us feel so comfortable. The reality was that we were living on overtime income, which is never a good idea, and we hit a financial wall as soon as the overtime pay lessened.

After finally getting our son off to college and on solid ground, we began focusing on what we thought would be a simple medical procedure for my wife. However, during that procedure, the doctor made a mistake that almost cost my wife a kidney and, at one point, her life, as the effects of the surgical mistake didn't show up right away. It wasn't until the pain from a kidney infection became unbearable that we recognized the seriousness of my wife's health condition.

This single mistake led to my wife having to endure six surgical procedures that included two visits to the emergency room, which turned into week-long stays in the hospital and a final week at a hospital in Maryland. The problem was corrected by the best doctor in this field of medicine. I was working no overtime at all because of my new work assignment, and I was right by my wife's side all the way through this life-threatening ordeal.

At this point, the accumulating bills were irrelevant, but I knew that I would have to face them at some point. I have never been the type of person to ask for help, and I was more than willing to endure this alone, which also proved to be a very stressful experience. I was responsible for taking care of my family; failing was not an option. The amount of time I could spend at work was limited, and I wasn't going to depend on anyone else to be by my wife's side during this time because she made it clear that having me by her side was healing for her.

I knew that after twenty-plus years of marriage and all the times my wife put everyone else first, it was time for me to show her my sacrificial love, and I was not going to let her down. It was during this vulnerable period that I realized just how much I needed my wife and how much I really love this woman. If it were possible, I would have taken the pain from her, but I couldn't, so I had to watch her suffer through it, which was extremely tough.

She has been and still is my God-sent lifeline; to be without her would have been devastating to me, so I took full advantage of the opportunity to do for her what she has done for me every day of our marriage.

In summary, I put her first. After the final checkup and visit to the hospital in Maryland about three weeks after spending a week-long stay to repair the mistake made by the first doctor, we were finally on the road to recovery. Now, we had to face what it would take to begin our journey of financial recovery, starting with the accumulation of doctors' bills.

I was not looking forward to facing this valley of obstacles, but I knew I would have to address the bills sooner or later. Without us even asking, my mother-in-love gave us much-needed financial support that allowed us to breathe for a moment. She was also more than willing to spend time with my wife and provide bedside support, but I knew this was a job I could not pass on to my mother-in-love. I truly thank God because my mother-in-love has been a pillar of support and guidance throughout our marriage.

The bills added up fast, and before we knew it, we were three months behind on our mortgage as well as everything else and found ourselves playing a financial juggling act. This was nothing like what we experienced in our earlier years of marriage. We found ourselves facing a short sale on our home or having to go through foreclosure. I didn't want either option initially because I felt like we could recover before we reached the point of no return on our house, but fighting to do that meant we couldn't save any money either. The material things became irrelevant compared to peace of mind and stress-free living. A short sale proved to be the best option for us because we didn't want to stay in the house forever anyway.

I saw the financial challenges approaching before missing any payments, which we hadn't done since we purchased the home, so I reached out to the financial institutions well in advance. But it was like everything lined up to create the perfect financial storm, forcing us to make a tough but necessary decision. The financial institute that held our mortgage loan wouldn't even consider us for an assistance program unless we were behind on our mortgage. This led us down the path of allowing our mortgage payment to be late in the first place. We followed the instructions of the financial institution's representatives, who explained how the assistance programs worked. My pride was on the line in my mind, so I was willing to get a second job if necessary, but that just didn't seem to make sense to me. When I accepted the fact that we were living on overtime pay, I knew a change was necessary.

I was told that I was up for promotion at my job and there was a good chance that I would be selected for a leadership position, so we passed up the first chance to take a short sale offer because I was thinking pridefully and didn't want to lose the house that way.

We never expected anything like this to happen to us, but it did, and we had to make some tough decisions. We decided to gain control of our financial stability, track everything coming and going through our hands, and then determine what we needed and didn't need, which allowed us to cut away some things to reduce our expenses. After doing that, we realized that we still couldn't save like we needed to for any future unplanned events.

It was by the grace of God that we were able to pass up the first short sale offer and restructure our loan, which allowed us to make up for the setback on the backend of the loan. However, that wouldn't allow us to save any money, so upon further review, we decided to pursue the short sale. This was no easy process, either, because there was a risk that we could lose the house to foreclosure if no one purchased it. Amazingly, within two months of having our house on the market, we had an offer on the table, and the financial institution had to accept the short sale offer. By the grace of God, we had acquired the services of an angel in our eyes who connected us with the right people.

My pride quickly became irrelevant because we would either be house-poor or financially stable, and at the end of the day, financially stable is what gave peace of mind to all of us. I thank God that my wife has never been attached to any material things and would give them all up if that meant we could live life comfortably. That made it easy to make the right decision for our family and sell our home to prevent foreclosure.

The craziest part was that I was promoted two weeks after signing the paperwork to complete the sale of our home. Even with the job promotion, though, we knew we had made the right decision for our family. I truly believe God was restructuring our thinking to position us for something better.

I thank God every day for re-aligning my thoughts because while my wife was more than willing to make the necessary adjustments, I had to be convinced. If I hadn't, we would have remained unprepared for any financial storms or, worse yet, unprepared for opportunities to help someone else.

It's been more than eight years since we sold that home, and what a relief it's been for us with that stress factor removed from our lives. After enduring the journey through the valley of recovery, we have restored our credit, paid off our debts, and regained an appreciation for the little things in life again.

The journey has been worth every lesson because knowing that my wife is healthy at the end of the day and having her matters more to me than anything else. After living in her brother's townhouse for four years and working extremely hard, we purchased a home again in a beautiful neighborhood that exceeded our imaginations. I thank God for a renewed mind!

That season of humility and restoration proved to be the greatest challenge for us as a family to date. We learned exactly what it means to be one tragic event away from extreme financial struggle when unprepared. This has led us to truly appreciate life more than material things, understand how important it is to sacrifice and save for unpredictable challenges, and the importance of seizing the opportunity to capitalize on a great deal. We recently sold our last home and are now debt-free by the grace of God. Thank you, God!

CHAPTER 23

A Mother's Love

When I think about my mother-in-love, it becomes overwhelmingly clear that she was destined to be an incredible mother. She is the ultimate example of a mother who shows unconditional love toward not only her children but also to whomever she crosses paths with. She provides guidance and mentorship to so many of her friends, family members, and young adults who embrace her love; when you encounter her love, you never want to let it go.

I am so thankful that God has allowed me to have such a loving mother as my mother-in-love. The characteristics of a "Mother's Love" that immediately come to mind for me are the unconditional love and sacrificial love expressed by mothers who put their children first. It is without question that my mother-in-love has dedicated her life to these two characteristics, and she leaves the stamp of a "Mother's Love" on everyone she touches. What is so amazing about my mother-in-love is that her mother died while giving birth to her, and I believe she became the mother to others that she had always wanted to have growing up.

While she was blessed to be raised by her grandmother, there is nothing like experiencing the nurturing of your own mother. Please understand that this is no disrespect to my own mother, but it is a reality for me. My mother had no desire to be a nurturing mother; she always described us as a burden that she yearned to get rid of as soon as she got the chance.

Nevertheless, God provided and protected me from total destruction during my journey as a child and has allowed me to experience the support and love of a mother who has been an angel.

She has no idea what goes on inside of me when she tells me that she loves me and that she's proud of me. Hearing those words from someone credible has been the missing piece for me because of what I remembered hearing from my mother. It still comes up from time to time that she said I would be nothing but a no-good bastard just like my father, because that was always the driving force for me to excel and gave me fuel to prove her wrong.

Now, my mother-in-love always gives me the support I need, and she lets me know when I am on the right track or when I need to make some adjustments. She has loved me as her son, and I thank God for her every day. The thing that makes it so different is the fact that I can feel the love of my mother-in-love through the way she delivers her words, and I know it is genuine, even when she's giving a message of correction. God is awesome!

In the beginning, I didn't know how to take or appreciate a mother's love because it wasn't what I experienced growing up. At first, I had convinced myself that my mother-in-love was simply extending her love to me because I was married to her daughter. That would have been fine, too, but she quickly put that to rest with her actions of genuine love toward me many times over. I was still a young man who needed a mother's love when my wife and I got married because there was so much to learn as a husband and a father. Even though I made mistakes along the way, I always received encouragement and love from my mother-in-love. Her words and actions began to fill a void in my life that I thought would never be filled by anyone, and it took a long time to accept that I was wrong. But God will supply all our needs!

Remember, in high school, I was an athlete who

excelled and received many awards, but I never heard "I'm proud of you" from my own mother, and my father was nowhere to be found. Even though my sister would tell me that she was proud of me from time to time, it just wasn't the same as my parents telling me because I wanted them to be proud of my accomplishments.

I married my wife at the age of twenty-two, shortly after graduating from the Newport News Apprentice School, but I was still learning how to be a man and father by way of trial and error. If I could paint a picture of my mother-in-love, it would look like an angel from heaven carrying me over a bridge from being a young adult into manhood. What I look like in the picture now is a father and husband standing strong, willing and committed to lay down my life for my family.

My mother-in-love's sacrificial actions were endless during that critical time of my life, and the only way I can truly pay her back is by taking care of her daughter and loving her grandchildren unconditionally and sacrificially, which is the least I can do. It's like she prepared me for the ultimate victory in life, and now I feel like I am the richest man on earth as I enjoy my family.

I love my mother-in-love, who has always treated me as a son and never as a son-in-law. In my eyes, she is the mother of all mothers and is an inspiration to everyone she meets—there are many others who have similar stories about her.

I always loved my own mother, but keeping it real, if she told me that she loved me—which was rare—I found it so hard to believe because her actions over the years said something totally different. From a visual standpoint, it was like looking at words come out of someone's mouth and watching those words fall to the floor right in front of the person they were trying to reach.

In conclusion, my mother-in-love has been the nurturing and encouraging mother in my life that every child needs to become the best they can be. I love and adore my mother-in-love because she has shown me every day what a mother's love looks and feels like.

Although my own mother worked very hard to drive me as far away from herself as she could, I still loved and prayed for her until she passed.

I rarely ask my mother-in-love for anything, and she doesn't give me a chance to ask because she always checks on me, and it's like she knows exactly when to tell me that she loves me and is proud of me. In a nutshell, it feels natural and easy for me to call my mother-in-love, but I had to force myself to call my own mother. Unfortunately, that is a reality for many when it comes to having a damaged relationship with one or both biological parents.

Nonetheless, I thank God for my mothers: the one who gave birth to me and my mother-in-love who has truly shown me a mother's love.

CHAPTER 24

The Apology

To my brother-in-love, who I love and appreciate more than words can express, I wish to offer an apology.

I had an emotional flashback with him as if he were my older brother one day many years ago. You see, he had done something that bothered me which could have been resolved so easily with a simple conversation. But I was so ready to turn that physical confrontation switch on because I didn't trust my own family since the family I had grown up with inflicted so much pain. I'd been primed to think that I had to protect myself all the time in every situation, so I responded as if all families were the same, and the only way I knew to deal with any disagreement was through physical confrontation. Not only was I wrong, but the awesome relationship we had was severely impacted in that single moment; he couldn't believe that I would even consider being physical with him. It's not that he couldn't handle himself; I just think he was so disappointed and hurt in that moment because we were not in-laws in his eyes, we were brothers, and he wasn't raised in an atmosphere where he had to fight his family members.

I have apologized since then, but that moment had a lasting impact because it occurred at least seven years before the initial release of the pain inside of me, and it wasn't until a few years ago that I was able to speak about what I experienced at the hands of my older brother. Even though I have been stronger than many as a father, husband, and family member, I made many mistakes along the way. But God is so amazing because He has kept me and those around me from experiencing a major family fall out.

As of today, God has restored our relationship and made it even stronger; we can count on each other for anything. For a season after my error, we conducted ourselves more like in-laws because of that one moment. We never got physical with one another; it was just a brief moment with a serious look of confrontation. I was in the place that I was conditioned to be in, not where I should have been mentally during that time, and

I made a family mistake that I had to apologize for. I have had to learn how to love my family the right way in all situations. It's been at least fifteen years since that occurred, so to my brother-in-love, I apologize, and I love you to life. You are an incredible man, and I admire and appreciate you.

I have witnessed over the years what a loving family looks like by observing my wife, my brother-in-love, and my mother-in-love. You won't find a family that's more loving than they are because they truly value the little things as well as the most important thing: the quality time spent with each other. We have moments of laughter that can truly heal a person like medicine because those moments are so full of love and joy. God has given me everything I need to succeed, including a loving family I can appreciate. We may not get a chance to replay a scenario that went the wrong way, but we can and should always apologize once we realize that we made a mistake. Thank you, God, for another chance.

PART 4

A Family Learning from the Past

Me and my son, Brian Jr.

CHAPTER 25

The Family Effect

Although we've been blessed to be a family of love and strength, we have had our own internal moments of struggle, and we are willing to share them in an effort to help others.

My mother passed on her anger, and my father gave me his irresponsibility. My father told me one day when my children were less than five years old that I was yelling in my house just like my mother, which I absolutely did not want to duplicate, so I stopped immediately. But of course, that was just one thing that was brought to my attention. I cringed at the thought of there being more, but for my family's sake, I was willing to accept what I looked like and be strong enough to do something about it. God can help us overcome anything.

My wife told me in my early years of disciplining our children that I was doing it in anger and not in love. At first, I didn't agree because I would sacrifice my life for them, but she was referring to my facial expressions and body language that said something else. Remembering what my father said about yelling and what my mother looked like when she disciplined us as children made me realize that I had to consider what my wife was saying about my facial expressions when I disciplined our children.

You see, when my mother would discipline us, it was like she hated our existence and wanted to kill us in those moments. Remember, I watched my mother viciously choke my sister one day because she ran up the phone bill making long-distance phone calls. Now, I never handled my children like that, nor would I ever put my hands on their faces. In fact, I never allowed them to hit each other or play in each other's faces, but I would spank their behinds when necessary. However, when I did, there was no discussion before or after the discipline; I would just give them a spanking without showing any compassion, according to my wife's observation.

I began to hug my children and talk to them before and after the discipline to ensure I was expressing love toward them in every way possible in those moments when it was necessary to discipline them. Now, I didn't have to discipline them long because after a few times, all I would have to do was say that I would spank them, and that was enough to straighten them out. I thank God for my wife, who has always balanced me. With those changes, I found myself doing more talking and less spanking.

I remember one day, my son had done something wrong in school that was bad enough for my wife to call me to carry out disciplinary actions on him. However, I was still at work, so he had to wait all day for the discipline that was supposed to be coming his way, and you know it's ten times worse on the child when they are waiting for the discipline.

When I finally made it home after working a twelve-hour day, you could feel the worry in the house and concern by all for Brian Jr., so I put my stuff down and told Brian to meet me in our bedroom. I talked to him for a few minutes, then tried to catch him off guard and swiftly tagged him in the chest with the back of my open hand because he was now in high school, and I thought he could handle that. I soon realized that I had knocked the wind out of him. He was gasping for air, and it scared the fool out of me. I did everything I could to help him regain his breath. Thank God he recovered quickly, even though it felt like forever. All I could think about in that moment was my son getting hurt or worse by my own hands. Again, it scared the mess out of me, so I declared that day that I would only use my heavy hands to embrace my children.

To see my son gasping for air like that because of my own actions was a total reminder of the abuse that I experienced as a child. To think that I could have hurt my son like that brought me to a place of internal remorse. My! My! My! It wasn't that my children ever questioned my love for them; it was the fact that I had them believing that I would physically harm them if they did something wrong that required discipline. I had imposed fear on my children by using a scared-straight tactic and hoping my children would do the right things out of fear of doing something wrong.

I do believe in disciplining your children, but there is a right way to do that, and being physical with your hands is not the answer. In fact, if it's not within the guidelines of the law, it can very easily be considered child abuse.

These lessons are not easy ones to learn, nor are they easy to share, but trust me when I say that telling my story is necessary for myself and others because there are many folks who use abusive styles of discipline.

My mother once made me sit at the kitchen table and tried to force me to eat liver, which I could not stand. Having to endure a whipping along with hours of agony at that table, ready to throw up from the smell of that food, was a moment I will never forget, and to this day, I still don't eat liver.

As a parent, I made my son eat some sausage one day that he didn't like, and although I didn't spank him, I still threatened to do it, which was just as bad. He also experienced nausea, and he was at the table for almost an hour of agony. Of course, to this day, our son only eats a certain type of sausage because of that experience. I did let him off the hook, even though, in my mind, I thought I was teaching him to appreciate the meal that he had in front of him. That lesson is great in theory, but it still has to be delivered the right way.

My wife supported me but didn't always agree with things like this, so she would secretly intervene, and I am so glad that she did. If I had realized that I was duplicating my mother's actions, I would have stopped immediately. Today, my kids can joke about that day because I told them I was wrong and that it was not the way to handle your children when it comes to eating food.

My mother would also come into the house every day and find something to fuss about. With that as my example of a parent growing up, now that I was a parent, I would come home and find something to complain about, which, of course, made my family feel at times like they could never do enough to please me, and that wasn't a good place for any of us to be. My wife always cleaned up the little messes I made with our children and made sure that I went back and corrected my own errors when I was willing to listen. At times, I think my wife felt like she was raising me to be the man I could be.

My mother had scrambled for money all her life, and any extra money she had would always go toward her pleasures first, then she might share whatever crumbs were left with us on a rare occasion. This really came to light after my mother inherited money from one of our aunts who passed away. Not that she was obligated to give anything to her children, but it just seemed like it would have been an instant reaction for a parent who cares for their children, at least in my mind.

I thought she would at least do something for her grandchildren because she hadn't spent much time with them at all. Now, she did give a thousand dollars to my siblings and me from what I understand. Of course, I ended up giving it to my children because I really didn't want anything from my mother other than a conversation filled with answers that would help me be a better person. Just saying!

As I look back over my life, I realize that I have duplicated the same actions of feeling like I had to be the first one to enjoy or reap the benefit from extra funds that came into the house. If we got a new car or something, I would be the one to fully enjoy it first, then my wife. I was just downright selfish and didn't realize why, nor did I understand how impactful those acts were on my family because my wife has always been content with whatever she has. She deserves nothing less than everything from me for all that she means to me and has sacrificed for our family.

These may not have had a huge negative impact on my relationship with my family, as they were just characteristics about me that they accepted and were overshadowed by my stance as a supporting father and a loving husband. But they are still things that I don't want to pass on to my children. Even so, when I think about it, my children are selfish to a degree and feel entitled to things because I gave them the things I didn't receive as a child without teaching them the principle of earning the things you get in life.

My wife had to endure some of the selfishness and irresponsible characteristics I displayed early in our marriage—until God corrected me. Prior to that change, she was solid as a rock in keeping us balanced as a family. I am an example of "behind ever good man is a great woman," and I can tell you that my wife is truly a "virtuous woman" because she has always been a hard worker and willing to sacrifice herself for the benefit of others.

My father displayed irresponsibility by leaving my sister and me without guidance and financial support, to the point of going to jail one time just so he wouldn't have to pay child support to our mother. We only saw him a couple of times growing up, and it was funny because in those moments, he displayed himself as "Mr. Big Shot" by taking us out to eat with money he really should have given to my mother in support of us.

As a father, I embraced paying child support for my oldest daughter. I had her at the age of nineteen, and I unfortunately repeated the cycle of not having all my children with one woman, but I refused to follow my father's footsteps by abandoning my daughter, so I paid the child support and remained a supporting father in my daughter's life. I love and adore her and my four grandchildren. The most important thing for me has been keeping my voice with my children to provide those nuggets of experience and guidance to them when they really need it.

You see, the tears of release I avoided by not discussing my past caused me to duplicate the actions of my parents and pass the pain on to my family. What I kept inside, thinking that I could just tough it out, still had a negative impact on the family I love and would sacrifice myself for, so that's why I am telling it all now.

The benefit of telling my story is that I have faced the fear of my past and identified the defensive actions I had taken to avoid the pain of revisiting those tough moments. To improve myself and help my family, I had to face the source of my internal struggle and allow God to help heal my heart and renew my mind.

I thank God for my wife, who kept telling me to write my experiences down in a journal because it would help me overcome my story within. Writing it down has proven to be very therapeutic for me in a way I would have never imagined. It took a while before I could write some of these emotional moments down on paper because it was like going back in time and facing those painful experiences. However, after getting over the pain of those memories, I began to heal on the inside, and that has started to show up on the outside. I have begun to enjoy life more and appreciate every day as I seek the good in others and the positive things in every situation. God is so amazing.

Sharing my past has really helped my family gain a much better understanding of me and has helped me see myself better, allowing me to self-improve. And yes, it is without question that I've had to ask for forgiveness along the way as I realized what I looked like at times and what my children experienced. I thank God for my wife because she has always been strong enough to confront my bad actions whenever I came close to being in error.

I am so committed to loving my family and finding ways to put smiles on their faces every chance I get because that is the least I can do. After all, my first responsibility is to my family. The dysfunction that I experienced as a child is not meant to be transferred to anyone else, which means I must stay the course, be transparent, and be vulnerable.

CHAPTER 26

My Children

What a journey! My firstborn child saved my life by causing me to think differently. I was on a road of self-destruction, and at nineteen, I had to decide to consider the life of my child above my own. My choices were reckless and not those of a parent, and it didn't take me long to realize that I was going to abandon my child if I didn't change. That's what I mean when I say that my oldest daughter saved my life; she gave me a reason to live.

I was at a crossroads in life; I was going to live or die, and I knew it. My firstborn led me to be there as a father, to provide for her and protect her like a father should.

After making the right decision as a father during that

window of time, I learned that my children are a reflection of me, including my good and bad habits. My son gave me a reason to stand strong as a man of standards and responsibility because I wanted to be the example to him that I had yearned to see growing up. The feeling of being left behind by a parent created a deep wound for me, and many of the scars I bear are the result of his absence. My nephew, who grew up with our children, gave me a reason to keep reaching and teaching others because he would pick up the lessons faster than my children and help them understand things better than I could explain to them at times. My nephew paid attention to every lesson and appreciated every family moment. My baby girl gave me a reason to be faithful to my wife as an example to her. My baby girl has been the ultimate protector of her parents' relationship and has passionately expressed to us how she values our love for one another, which inspires her to love others the same way. What a gift!

I love and adore them, and I am so blessed to be here to enjoy my grandchildren. The one thing I did right was keeping my voice with my children, and I need to thank my wife for helping me do that. Sometimes, we can be so tough on our children that we push them away with no desire to return, not even for a brief visit. At times, I was hard on them and it made them uncomfortable, but my wife has always been there to clean up my messes and lovingly correct me before my mistakes caused irreparable damage.

CHAPTER 27

A Season to Remember

God made a way of escape through coaching others, which gave me the opportunity to channel my energy in a positive direction. Of course, it was my wife who said that I should coach our son in basketball on the sideline instead of coaching from the bleachers because I knew the game—or so I thought since I had accomplished much as a player in high school and finished my basketball career scoring more than sixteen hundred points at the Newport News Apprentice School. I must say that coaching inside the box on the sideline is not as easy as it looks because the information you give the players has to be positive and proactive—not reactive—if you are going to win. Usually, parents who yell from the bleachers are telling kids what to do *after* the fact rather than before it happens.

So, I left the bleachers and plunged into the coaches' box on the sideline. I started training our son and many other players during this journey, which also had the benefit of helping me become a better father because I had to use methods other than physical contact to instill discipline, structure, and good habits in the players. This journey also gave me a better understanding of how to deal with people because it forced me to interact with parents and players from all over.

Now, this is where my internal struggle began to show up as my strength. It was so fulfilling to stand in the gap as a father and mentor because it felt like I was going back in time to protect and cover myself as a father. I thank God for Coach Baggett, who stood in the gap for me and showed me the way. Because he didn't want anything in return, I strove to pay it forward by helping as many others as I could.

After embracing the push to coach from my wife, the journey began with recreational league teams, coaching girls and boys. This was so much fun because it allowed me to transfer my adversity-conquering mentality to others, starting with my own children. My wife and I would cover each child as needed, whether it was providing clothing, food, rides, mentoring, care, or covering them with prayer. We did this for at least two years on a recreational level before we transferred our efforts to competitive youth basketball with the Amateur Athletic Union (AAU).

This is where the journey to the championship began, but before reaching that goal, we had to learn the value of discipline, the need for structure, and the importance of having good habits. While learning to coach basketball, I took many lumps myself because everything changes when you stand in that coaches' box. The first thing I gained was respect for all the coaches courageous enough to stand in that box. The one thing I had no issue with was outworking and outlasting the competition, but to win a championship, I had to learn and coach the players to consistently do things the right way.

I was now in a position to be a supportive father and committed mentor to a group of young men who just needed someone to believe in them and another chance to compete. We had kids with two parents, one parent, or no parents at all, and they had many humbling stories of their own. Being there for the kids was like giving myself the guidance I yearned for as a youth with love and encouragement to go along with it.

While I was learning how to coach, the players learned how to overcome their own adversity. I taught them how to be adversity killers with relentless effort and determination, going beyond the wall of mental fatigue to become the best of the best and pushing them beyond their mental limits.

Basketball was the tool used to teach these players about overcoming life's obstacles with the right attitude. Some of the parents would call during the week for help with their kids because I had become the voice of discipline to them; all I had to say was do your homework or home assignment, and it was done. I had earned the kids' respect by caring for them first and encouraging them to be their best every day and everywhere.

When we started on the court, we lost games by thirty points to teams that weren't that good but had structure, an understanding of the principles, and the right habits during the game, which helped them win—for example, boxing out as a team, making free throws, using bounce passes and ball fakes, running simple plays, and understanding how to apply full-court pressure and how to beat full-court pressure. No matter what team it was, they all won by doing the same things, and the teams that played the hardest doing those things usually won the game.

When I first stood in the coaches' box, the game moved at warp speed, and everything I told the players was reactive to what the other teams were doing, which usually meant it was too late. I knew we played harder than any other team, but we were still learning how to put it all together, so we took many lumps. My mentor coach told me one day that watching me coach early on was like watching somebody run into a wall over and over as hard as they could with an open door just five feet away from them. What a rough thing to hear! However, he also said my passion and energy couldn't be contained. I later became his head assistant coach for the boys' high school varsity basketball team, where we won many games and made history along the way.

There were moments of tears due to some tough losses along this journey, but we developed as a unit, and I was given the opportunity to transfer my strength to overcome adversity. For the most part, the players knew nothing about the struggles that shaped me into the adversity killer I am today, but I did share a few of my challenges with them to make a point from time to time.

This journey gave me unexplainable joy because I could see the players and my children becoming adversity-conquering warriors. I feared no one, and neither did they; the thing about these kids was that they just needed someone to believe in them. It took some time to gain their trust, but I knew how to communicate with them to gain their trust because I knew what it took to reach me: believing in them, encouraging them beyond their mistakes, listening to them when they just needed an ear, but most of all, giving them the embrace of a father when necessary.

After a few seasons of enduring losses, we began to

put the pieces together and started winning games, but we couldn't defeat the best teams in the country yet. It wasn't until I accepted the challenge of becoming a champion as a coach that I was able to transfer this mentality to the players because they were feeding off of me, and they could see the belief or doubt in me during crunch-time moments that went far beyond my words.

To me, this is the final piece to becoming the champion or remaining a runner-up: the coach's ability to transfer his belief in that critical moment of the game when it's all on the line. Otherwise, the team will play off your doubt. Discipline, structure, and good habits can be in place, but belief in the critical moment takes you to the winner's circle.

In 2005, we finished fourth in the state and made it to the national tournament but lost in pool play, so we played the supplemental tournament and lost in the second round. The next season, we finished second in the state and made it out of pool play in the nationals, only to lose again, coming up short of a prize. 2007 was the year of completion for us. I had become a coach who believed our team belonged in the winner's circle. We had overcome many obstacles along the way and were ready to compete with anybody. We had started defeating teams older than us, which declared that the boys were strong enough to compete with the top teams in the country.

We committed to being disciplined, we had a solid team structure, and the players were on auto-pilot with good habits. Even the parents played their part without distracting the players as they began to see the value of team order. Teams we had lost to in the past, we now beat by as much as fifty points, so we had to play older teams to bring out the best in the players. The players were ready and deserved to win, and this would prove to be a season to remember.

The state tournament was the first big test. After beating a tough team from Norfolk (one of the best teams in the country; they had finished fifth overall in the nation just two seasons prior) to get to the semi-finals, we finally made our way to the winner's circle, beating that same team the next day by more than thirty points.

As the coach, I had developed a method of going a hundred miles an hour and going a hundred yards past the finish line. During the State Championship game, the referee had to tell me that we were up by thirty points with six minutes left because the clock and scoreboard were at the scorer's table. One of the players on the opposing team now plays in the NBA, so they were tough. It's hard to tell players not to play hard once you get them on this level, especially against an opponent we'd lost to for years. We won the game with great sportsmanship. We embraced the moment after winning the State Championship, and when we took the team picture, my facial expression displayed the intensity I was feeling in that moment because in my mind, I was still running past the finish line.

Having won the State Championship, we were in a different position going into the national tournament, which at the time contained at least ten players who currently play in the NBA. We started by winning our pool after beating the top team out of Chicago, Illinois, a team that we were losing to at halftime by seventeen points. All those battles against the older teams paid off. That same team still finished in the top ten at nine out of one hundred sixty teams playing for the National Championship.

Unfortunately, I was suspended before the first game of the tournament after winning the pool because I missed a tournament team meeting—totally an oversight on my part—but the players were so prepared that we won the game with me yelling from fifty feet away; it was an amazing win. God was all in this journey. Talk about transferring belief! We lost our second game of the tournament though, to a team that had won the National Championship two years earlier.

After losing that game, we couldn't win the National Championship, but we still had a chance to come home with some hardware. We went on to win the next three games in overtime. In one, my son, Brian Jr., hit a sixty-footer to put us in overtime. In the next game, Chaz

Robinson, who normally takes that game-changing charge or gets that backside rebound that determines the outcome of the game, hit a three-pointer, which turned out to be a game-winner. After seven wins and one loss, we found ourselves in a placement game, which meant we were going home with hardware for seventh or eleventh place. This was an incredible accomplishment because every team in the top fifteen that year was just one win away from playing for the title.

Out of all the teams in the tournament, our opponent was the best team out of the Baltimore/DC/Maryland area. We had never defeated them, and two years prior to this tournament, they played the team that had just beaten us two days earlier in the National Championship. We had recorded at least four losses to them over the years, losing by thirty points more than once. The coach was someone I looked up to because of how hard his team played and how great a coach he was for the kids.

But this game was different because I believed that we belonged in the winner's circle, and so did my players. Our opponent had just beaten the best team out of Philadelphia and Maryland prior to this game, which matters because teams from these areas usually played harder than any other teams in the country. But remember, we feared no one, and there was no doubt that we were tough enough to beat any team in this tournament.

The coaches and I greeted each other with an embrace of love and respect, but they knew I was dialed in as a coach and refused to allow any distractions to interfere with us achieving our goal. To me, defeating them would be far greater than winning the championship because they could have very easily been the defending national champions, and the fact that we had never defeated them would make this the ultimate achievement.

We played against them better than any other team had all season, and when the buzzer sounded, we were holding up a trophy for seventh place out of one hundred sixty teams, beating them by eleven points. It was a tough game because the players on both teams had a refuse-to-lose mentality. The coach usually got into the head of the opposing coaches, but I knew their strategy, so I didn't fall for it. I took away their strength, not allowing them to run their fast break, which is how they dominated teams along with relentless defensive ball pressure, and we also walked through their press with ease. At the conclusion of the game, the coach gained control of his team's emotions, and he and his team embraced us with brotherly love.

It was incredible; this was a moment filled with "Tears of Joy" because teams go years without reaching this goal, and some never do. It was another moment for overcoming adversity, and I knew that I had become one of the best youth coaches in the country. We all learned how to channel our energy into achieving something positive, crossing that bridge of potential to reach the place of a champion. This achievement was just as big for me as it was for them because I'd made it to the winner's circle as a coach. I still remember the referees telling me after the games that they thoroughly enjoyed our games. You see, we were so disciplined that we didn't focus on the referees at all because we were committed to playing the games the right way and playing harder than the other teams.

Even the gentleman running the tournament embraced me after he handed me the trophy for seventh place because he knew that we didn't miss the team meeting on purpose, and that meeting had resulted in over fifty coaches being suspended. We, "The Hampton Hoyas," out of the 757, were the underdogs who believed we could win. I even received phone calls after each game we won from our area AAU CEO. It was just amazing. God was all over this journey.

After this incredible journey, these kids went on to high school. They took this experience with them, which led to district and state championships and allowed some to receive basketball and football scholarships as a result of their efforts. Today, several of them are college graduates and productive in society. My prayer for them now is that they continue to become productive young men, mentors, coaches, and supportive fathers in life. My favorite sayings as a coach were "Let's Grind" and "We are Adversity Killers." Some of the kids have put these sayings on their bodies as tattoos. I still follow and support them, and I probably will for as long as God allows; they are our children for life.

I thank God for allowing me the opportunity to become a productive role model as a husband and father figure to more than my own while coaching, training, and mentoring kids on a journey that led to the experience of "a Season to Remember."

CHAPTER 28

Forgiveness in Action

As I journeyed with God, I realized that I'd been contained by the pain in my mentally created box of protection, preventing myself from trusting others enough to let them into my inner circle, including fully trusting God. I became content living in a world of internal isolation, which hindered me from walking in my full potential and authenticity.

It wasn't until I was ready to release the pain inside me by sharing my story with others that I would reach the doorway of forgiveness for the people who had inflicted emotional and physical harm on me. I now realize it's a process we must go through to experience healing and overcome the impact of those traumatic moments.

God has allowed me to enjoy the family I dreamed of having, and the more I think about my past, the more I realize that my experiences gave me the determination to come home every day to ensure I never let my wife and children down. Even though our children are older now and my wife and I have been married for more than thirty years, we still greet each other at the door with a hug and a kiss and express excitement at seeing one another every day.

Forgiveness, to me, means freedom from the box of limitations we build in our minds, allowing us to move forward in life doing what we've been blessed to do.

God sends the right folks our way at the right times to ensure we fulfill our purpose, and the key is that we must be willing to receive as well as respond to the wise instructions we're given from those individuals.

I've been blessed at my job to be a part of a team selected to lead change and improvement, which has forced me to expand my thinking about my platform of promise. While being the transparent person that I am, along with having the favor of God, I find myself in the presence of the decision-makers responsible for an entire organization. I receive personal mentoring from the top officials, and they've all given me a similar message: "You are better than you think, and your influence reaches far beyond your eyes."

God is so amazing, and He has opened doors that I

never even imagined going through. I now listen to my wife early and often, as well as my father, who can take the information I share with him about myself and clarify things for me about where I am and where I'm headed based on his own experiences and the fact that we have made similar decisions in life.

Then we were hit with a combination of mind-blowing favorable moments when my wife and I had to give up our home in 2014 in a short sale to regain control of our finances, and not even a full year later, we found ourselves in a position to save my mother from losing her home to foreclosure in 2015. Only God could arrange such a scenario.

This is where forgiveness goes beyond my thoughts. I listened to my wife, who prompted me to call my mother and find out how she was doing, which led to finding out that she was a week away from having to leave the house for good because the established foreclosure date was fast approaching. So, my wife and I were presented with the opportunity to help my mother. We immediately called the real estate agent who sold our home, and she stated that we couldn't do anything right then because of the existing guidelines for individuals who have gone through a short sale. She said to call back in two years, so I thanked the agent and quickly realized that this was a setup to experience the favor of God and exercise forgiveness.

You see, it took the power of God for me to even consider helping my mother in this situation, so I decided to see it through, and I knew God was all over this one.

My mother had a home that was paid for and decided to get a loan for one hundred and fifty thousand dollars. To assume this debt for her would be like giving her that money myself to blow. This just didn't make sense to me, but God's plan is much bigger than my emotional roadblock with my mother.

My wife's vision was far beyond mine on this one, and all she kept saying was "recompense," thanks to messages we received about experiencing the unexpected and restoration, which required our total trust in God. It was a setup.

My mother had also put my older brother on the deed, and he was set to inherit the property in the event of her passing, so that made this scenario even more unimaginable as far as me stepping in to help them after everything they had both done to me as a youth. Wow, God!

Again, I couldn't imagine this scenario in my wildest dreams or, better yet, my worst nightmare. The very folks who made me experience the worst moments in my life were the same ones my wife and I were positioned to save from foreclosure on this home. I believe the story of Joseph now more than ever.

Now, the loan conditions that my mother had at the bank were better than we could've received based on our current credit situation and even better than the one we had on our previous home. God was giving us something we couldn't receive on our own, leading us by our commitment to serving Him and a love that never fails into a situation that only He could work out. The bank normally doesn't utilize the loan assumption option, and the short sale rules are usually enforced, which means we wouldn't be able to purchase a home for two to three years after signing the short sale paperwork.

"But, God," is all we can say to this scenario because He blew up our imagination and exceeded our thoughts.

My mother was seventy years old and not in a condition to be moving at that stage of her life, but for us to absorb her debt seemed absurd to me. However, this property had been in our family since the early 1940s, and the thought of letting it go to foreclosure seemed even more absurd. God had to adjust my thinking to even consider doing this, and He did just that.

The process was short: removing my mother and brother from the existing deed, putting ourselves on the deed, and completing the loan assumption paperwork with the bank. God had it all worked out before we even considered helping my mother. I am just blown away by the very thought of this situation playing out like this because I was reminded of what my mother said over and over and how she had me put out of her house like it just happened yesterday.

That's how I know God has a real sense of humor because we usually think we know what we will do in certain situations, but God has a way of rearranging things, starting with our thoughts and then following through to our actions.

This scenario was set up to restore our finances and remove this debt from my mother so she wouldn't have to relocate at this stage of her life. This act broke the barrier of forgiveness toward my mother and older brother.

The bank stated that we were approved for the loan assumption based on our debt-to-income ratio because we had spent the last ten months paying off existing debts and saving money. My mother and brother signed over the deed as a gift, which was certified through a lawyer and the court. The next step was to sign the loan assumption paperwork to take complete ownership of the property.

Amazingly, we signed the paperwork, and my mother no longer had to move. My older brother was released from the burden of having a foreclosure on his credit report.

I told myself that God is truly in control, and I decided to trust God more than myself. What a mighty God we serve!

Even in my job, I have experienced favor beyond my imagination as one of the top officials in the program has made it his personal assignment to mentor me and encourage me to become the best I can be while influencing others to do the same. It is truly amazing what God can and will do when we accept that we don't have it all figured out and get out of His way with our thoughts and actions.

After rescuing my mother from being put out of the house as well as paying half of the mortgage payment so she could stay in the home, we also reduced her payment to $400, paid the remaining balance of $300 of the mortgage payment every month, and allowed her to stay in the home. My mother decided to leave the house three months later. She called to tell me that she would no longer make any more payments, left the house, moved into an apartment, and purchased a new car. My wife and I were stunned by her actions, as we were left with the challenge of figuring out how to make payments for two households. We now had our own residence and the debt of a home worth less than the loan on it.

We spent over twelve thousand dollars on that house to restore the foundation and rented the home to a God-sent man who desired to purchase the property. Amazingly, the renter renewed the entire home on the inside, from replacing the plumbing to rewiring the house and replacing all interior walls. He was a man in need of a chance to restore his credit, and he kept his word every step of the way. This proved to me that God has a plan much bigger than ours, and we must learn to trust Him every step of the way.

Helping my mother also led me to do something that again blew my mind: giving my car to my youngest daughter when she had just turned twenty-one. With all that she has been through (which is her story to tell) and the fact that she has been a trooper through it all, I felt that she deserved something special. Now, this was a total shift for me because of my mentality with vehicles and the fact that I was in no position to get another vehicle at the time, but I couldn't have made a better decision because my daughter has a heart to give, and she does it all the time.

Thank you, God, for yet again rearranging my thoughts and leading me to do something beyond my imagination.

As of today, the renter has finalized the purchase of the home we took over to prevent my mother from enduring a foreclosure, and we sold the home for the cost of the loan balance, which had been reduced to $118,000 due to payments over a period of four years. This was also a test to see if we would follow through with doing something for someone who could not do it themselves. We have earned a friend for life with the renter out of an act of kindness and the favor of God.

Thank you, God, for your grace and mercy.

CHAPTER 29

Closure and Relief

Last year, I had a discussion with my mother's best friend of more than forty years, Cynthia Robinson, and I received the closure that I longed for with my mother because she had a front-row seat to my experiences as a child. As she embraced me with a big hug and a strong message of "I love you," she began to tell me how hard it was for her to watch me go through the things I did as a child. She also told me that she wanted to take me away from my mother and raise me herself. I quickly realized that other people were well aware of our family struggles and my memories were not off the mark.

She explained to me that my mother never knew how

to love; all she knew was the violence of her own childhood. As I listened to Cynthia tell me about her decades of experiences with my mother, I began to feel sorry for my mother, and it gave me closure while relieving me of the internal struggle of yearning for my mother's nurturing love.

Cynthia brought me to tears with a statement: "It's okay to dream again; don't stop dreaming and believing in yourself." Her words released me from the mental prison created by my mother's words and fortified by my thoughts. Amazingly, I had the key to my mental prison the entire time, but I needed someone credible to tell me that it was time to leave that place and move on.

My wife continues to push me to be the productive person I am meant to be and accept the new season. Additionally, it has taken the last several years of coaching and encouragement from Stephen Fahey and the last two years of candid conversations with Gilda Stafford, who says, "Stop being afraid and move from what was, into what is, no longer speaking the words of a victim but living the rest of my life as a victor," to believe in my ability to lead others.

CHAPTER 30

Redirection

God will rearrange things for us sometimes to get us on a purpose-filled path in life that positively impacts others. After becoming a father and losing a close friend who was tragically shot and killed, I was drawn to God as I sought to become a better example to others in every area of my life. There was a period of time when I needed to follow a new path, and if I was going to accomplish my God-given assignment, I needed to have a strong woman at my side who not only complemented me but completed me.

I made myself predictable to my family so they knew where I was, what I was doing, and what I would and would not do. This may seem boring to some, but you have no idea how priceless peace of mind is. It just goes to show that God can do exceedingly and abundantly above all that we could ever ask or think according to His power that works in us. I was continuously told by my own mother that I would never be anything but a no-good bastard just like my father, and I believed it for a long time. That's why people should listen to the whole matter before giving their opinions about what someone else should do instead of telling them to just forget about it because that thing happened in their past. As a hurting individual, I needed to talk to someone credible, and my wife has proven to be that person time and time again.

Sometimes, the words spoken by the ones we rely on and expect to be loved by can and will impact our lives. I had to go through something to become the man I am, and it means everything to me to love my family the right way. I know it is by the grace of God that I didn't follow the examples in front of me. And yet, though I believed in God's amazing power for the longest time, it was hard for me to get past the doubt embedded in my thoughts. I would get to the door of my blessings and refuse to go through it because I couldn't get beyond my mother's words. I believed in everyone but myself, so I found myself always pushing someone else into that place God was assigning to me.

I understand now that it is my responsibility to walk in my purpose with the passion God gave me. What an incredible journey it has been thus far, and I am excited to have a mindset delivered from the strongholds of my past. There is a process we must go through to get to that place of deliverance, and there will be a few individuals God will send our way who will have that confirming message. We must reach a point where we can trust those who have our best interests at heart and are assigned to help us fulfill our purpose. God is amazing!

PART 5

From My Family to Yours

Me facilitating a discussion about leading by example with a room full of leaders from across the country.

The message? We lead people from our hearts, not fear.

CHAPTER 31

Helping Others

My wife and I have a passion for helping others see the priceless gifts they have within their families. In relationships, people too often settle for moments of pleasure that turn into broken homes and a lifetime of struggle instead of making the sacrifices that allow them to enjoy the fruits of their labor and experience the lifetime of success that comes through the expression of unconditional love toward others.

My wife and I have also extended ourselves to help children by giving them the support they need as well as a place to stay when necessary. For six years, we opened our home, at our own expense for most of that time, to help children in need. My wife grew up helping others; it has been her mother's lifetime passion to provide for children, whether they were hers or not, and my wife has taken that torch from her mother, along with the passion to carry it into the next generation.

As for me, it's like reaching back to help myself as a child in need. Sometimes, all people need is to know that someone cares. Life is full of obstacles, adversity, and feelings of doubt that work against our progress and overall success, so we must learn to be positive and believe in our ability to accomplish anything.

My wife and I have accepted our purpose in the kingdom of God to help other married couples see the importance of valuing each other every day and to be the best example we can be for everyone around us. The encouragement of our children pushes us to be a standard of excellence and drives our desire to give God our very best everywhere we go.

CHAPTER 32

Crossing the Bridge

From potential across promise and into purpose.

If there ever was a must-do in life for me, it's that I must accept my place, cross the bridge of promise, and step into the place of purpose made just for me. What I have realized is that right at the point of crossing the bridge into a purpose-filled life, I have historically looked back and stepped onto the same side of the vision instead of crossing over the bridge of promises. I have become a great encourager of those around me who needed a little push to get on the other side, but I have not been courageous enough to cross over into that unfamiliar territory myself.

Now, it seems like God has used my passion for

helping others as the tool to get me on the bridge, and the same folks I've been encouraging are giving it right back to me, not allowing me to stay on the same side of the vision. I am on the bridge, and I have crossed the midpoint. Now, the bridge has a gap in it, and I can no longer go backward to access the side known as potential. This means I must go through the lessons of the promise that clarify the assignment and embrace a life of purpose on the other side of the bridge.

I have struggled and turned back out of fear long enough, and this process has led me to become the authentic, energized, and unapologetic version of myself. I am so excited that I can finally accept the things God has for me without feeling bad about them or focusing on how my successes will make others feel, because those feelings kept me from stepping into that place of promise. Taking my place as a leader in my job and as a mentor in ministry and in the community is my form of crossing the bridge into the promises of God.

Crossing the bridge starts in our minds before it ever turns into actions, because we must first understand where we are and what has caused us to react to things the way we have in the past. Only then will we be in a better position mentally to accept the things God sends our way to take us to our destiny, which is a fulfilled life of purpose and productivity. God is awesome!

God has been preparing me for this moment,

regardless of my age and all the mistakes I've made along the way. It's like a puzzle that has been put together, and all the lessons have added up to a complete picture called "The Promises of God." I am excited about being energized, and the great thing is that the message for me has been to just be the best "ME" that I can be. Regardless of what other people do or have done to me, it has prepared me for the greater work I have in front of me.

God will lead us to our vision even though we may not physically see anything yet. We must trust God and the confirmation that He sends our way through others. Believing our way into the reality of our vision directs us straight into our destiny of living a fulfilled life that will benefit the person we see in the mirror and everyone connected to us.

I have made enough decisions that have allowed my family to experience only a portion of what God really has for us, and it is time to fully accept and embrace the favor of God.

I understand now that we all face a "bridge" moment in life, a moment where we can visualize the promised land and must trust God to get there. He will send the right folks our way to give us the assistance we need to reach our goals. The key is to keep our focus on God the whole way. If we put our trust in man, then we are sure to be let down simply because no one else will be given the same measure of faith we possess for the vision that God has given us.

At the foot of the bridge, we must decide to no longer give in to the fear of what we physically see with our eyes, because what we see is an incomplete picture. We must exhaust ourselves and utilize every ounce of energy we have, believing in the vision even when all others doubt. Without faith, it is impossible to please God, but if we believe and take action, all things are possible to him who believes.

God is waiting for us to accept Him through His Son Jesus Christ, walk in His love, enjoy the life He has given to us, and realize that our struggles will become our strengths. We must cross the bridge.

I was given the opportunity to participate in a leadership development program that has propelled me into that place of becoming the energetic me. I have interacted with some incredible people God has used to confirm His message to me. It is undeniably clear that as I've become the energetic me, I have truly begun to disregard the negative opinions of others because they are none of my business anyway. Huge thanks go out to my mentors for their support and words of inspiration; I truly believe God used them to help me understand how important it is to be myself with confidence, operate with no fear, and lead others with love every day.

As if that wasn't enough, I recently accepted the

opportunity to be the dean of a senior leader workshop, which is an assignment to lead leaders across the corporation. God has given me a platform to be a billboard as an authentic, energized, and unapologetic leader who encourages others to be the best version of themselves. God is so good.

CHAPTER 33

Learning to Love Yourself

To love ourselves, we must first learn to appreciate the love and grace God gives us, and we must return that love back to Him with all of our heart, mind, and soul, which is to accept, confess, and commit to serving Him by loving others.

What we receive in return is a light that can change lives when allowed to shine. We learn to love others without judgment or prejudice. This allows us to see and accept the areas of correction in our lives, helping us serve our families and everyone else around us.

We are expected to lay our lives down for our families every day as an expression of love because they are a part of us, and we cannot completely love ourselves without loving them. I am living proof because I have experienced both sides of this coin, first as a youth dealing with the issues of life after being abandoned by my father at six months and living through the pain of being raised by an angry mother, then by becoming a parent myself and trying to correct those mistakes. My wife and I have done our best to be parents who have made all the necessary moves to express that unconditional and sacrificial love toward our children. The rewards I have received are peace of mind and the blessings of God.

As such, I seek to understand what moves me, motivates me, angers me, makes me defensive, makes me feel positive or negative, makes me laugh or cry, and who or what has influenced me to feel the way I do about anything. Then, I decide if I want to continue down that path or change a few things to ensure that my actions will positively influence others. In a nutshell, I simply look in the mirror at myself and learn to love the person I see, along with my wife, children, and grandchildren.

CHAPTER 34

Looking in the Mirror

I am so excited about what God is doing in my life, and all that started with allowing myself to see what I truly look like in the mirror of life. It was not a pleasant picture at first glance, and I am not referring to my physical appearance; I am referring to who I am as a person and how I conduct myself when interacting with others.

The mirror experience gives us the opportunity to make the necessary changes that will not only improve our lives but help us become a much better example to others. My mirror isn't glass; it's my wife, children, family, coworkers, and friends. The purpose of the mirror experience is to improve our influence on others because our habits, whether good or bad, can and will become the habits of those we influence. For example, our children will walk and talk just like we do; they will make similar decisions when they are confronted with similar situations when dealing with people, choosing to help others, establishing good work ethics, or spending money, and their lives will be impacted by their decisions. The funny thing is that until we accept what we truly look like and decide to make changes to improve ourselves, we will continue to repeat the same lessons, and that means the people we influence will struggle with the same lessons until someone decides to do something different.

To receive the promises of God and reach our destinies in life, we must learn the lessons of life and begin sharing those lessons with others as an act of servanthood.

My wife and I have finally reached a point in life where we spend less and save more. What I have learned from my children over the years is that the most valuable gift I could ever give them is my time. Although we gave our children more material things than we had growing up, at the end of the day, they wanted our time more than anything. We recognize now as grandparents that our grandchildren want our time more than anything else—as well as the toys they are asking for! My wife was already there, so this was more of a lesson for me to learn because I am the leader of our household, and our children will follow my lead. If I don't get this part right, our children will likely repeat the same mistakes with their children until they have a life-changing mirror moment.

In the past, I would discipline our children without having a discussion with them until my wife helped me clean my mirror; then, I shifted to talking their ears off before and after disciplining them. I am learning to listen to them more, seeking to understand where they are mentally, and giving them words of encouragement more than correction. When done correctly, they are thankful for the conversation and, I hope, wiser for it.

CHAPTER 35

Wise Council

I truly understand now that every dream or vision comes to life with the assistance of others. The Bible calls this a wise council, and businesses call them board members, council members, or even a committee at times. The bottom line is that we cannot be an island all to ourselves because we need the help of others to complete the vision we are made for. Our God-given assignment will always include helping or doing for others; after all, that's the reason we were given the vision in the first place.

Your wise council usually confirms the message that God has already given you or helps piece together all the different parts that make up the complete picture.

However, we must be careful of input from the wrong people because it can quickly become something others try to take over but fail to complete. After all, they do not have the measure of faith to see the vision God gave us come to life that we do. God provides us with the vision, desire, and endurance to carry the torch of goodness into the next generation, ultimately producing good fruit in the form of those who are productive in life and are committed to helping others.

Your circle of influence matters because we make decisions based on those around us who will amplify our faith or increase our fears. God has not given us the spirit of fear but one of power, love, and a sound mind. People tend to speak about their own fears, and at times, they unintentionally transfer those fears to others around them. Members of your wise council will uplift you, encourage you, inspire you, and confirm the message you initially received from within. Those within your wise council have the ability to energize you with their presence and words. These select individuals will also tell you the absolute truth, even when you don't want to hear it, because their love is authentic and they have your best interest at heart.

To all, I encourage you to choose your circle wisely and be willing to embrace the encouragement and correction you receive from your wise council. Huge thanks to my wise council of Rodney Pierce, Travis

Parker, Keith McKoy, and my father, Mathew "Tinee" Darden.

CHAPTER 36

Embracing Leadership

The day I embraced the role of leadership was the day I faced one of my toughest moments with someone I supervised. My day started early, and I was playing a song of encouragement as I entered my office. This particular morning, two of my staff members were in an adjacent office, and one person decided to use some unprofessional words to tell me to turn my music off. Without thinking twice, I found myself in that office, firmly addressing this individual with intense passion, and I let him know that he had one more time to disrespect me before I would deal with him myself.

Getting physical with any employee was not an option, but this guy continued to push the envelope until it reached a tipping point with me. He challenged my faith, and in my mind, he was coming against the God I serve. After the firm conversation, the gentleman understood how serious this moment had become, and he knew that he had gone too far. I had to go into my office, close the door, and sit for the next twenty minutes. I realized that I was not in complete control of my emotions. After much thought, I realized the lesson was mine and not his because the gentleman was just being himself, and this was a moment for me to embrace the next level of leadership.

This moment proved to be one of my best lessons. Thirty minutes later, I called the gentleman into my office to clear the air and discuss what happened. I started by apologizing to him because I was responsible for him and the entire team of more than four hundred employees. I let him know that I have no tolerance for someone using unprofessional language, especially if the words are directed at me. I shared my "why" with him, and he had a much better understanding of why I reacted the way I did. He apologized, said he meant no disrespect, and declared he would never do it again.

After talking with the gentleman for about an hour, I realized how important this lesson was for me because I had a team of employees with a low tolerance level for unprofessionalism. If I was going to lead others in a way that helps them get beyond their emotions and respond with intelligence, I had to learn this lesson first. So, I embraced this moment and committed to walking with this employee every day until I learned everything I could about getting beyond my emotions in an instant and making wise decisions.

Since that moment, the gentleman and I have talked every day about work, which has now transitioned into conversations about life. Only God could have orchestrated such a quick turn-around of events between two individuals who were at odds for a brief moment. I knew I had to embrace my role as a leader who can get beyond personal emotions and respond with intelligence during moments of adversity.

Today, the same employee comes to work excited about doing his job. I have positioned myself as a student to him, and he embraces every moment to share his knowledge with me. We both have pasts that contain moments of hardship, which has positively created our drive, but we recognize the fact that we still have broken pieces inside us that cause us to be defensive at times.

I learned one of my greatest lessons and have become a much better leader as a result of this moment. I must pause and reflect to allow myself to think first about the outcome of a bad decision and be able to respond intelligently. The gentleman has embraced the challenge of teaching other staff members everything he knows and has committed to helping me at any hour of the day. What a lesson!

Next-level leadership requires us to recognize that our employees' emotions are rarely, if ever, about us, and we must be able to control our own emotions in order to help the individuals we are assigned to lead. I realize that within the workforce and leadership, there are people who walk around every day with internal brokenness or areas they have not yet overcome in life. As a leader, I have learned to listen with my eyes and ears to hear the hearts of team members, which has helped me better understand their passions. This gives me the insight I need to make better decisions and provide better assistance for the employees I serve.

CHAPTER 37

Knowing Our Parents

It is critically important to understand the parents we came from because there are things we naturally inherit from them without even growing up in their presence. You see, not only do I look like my father, but I talk, sing, sit, and stand like him even though I wasn't raised by him. There are some things I do not want to pass on to my children, so I am committed to having as many conversations with my father as I possibly can so I can learn from his mistakes. I have faced some similar situations, and after having discussions with my father, I realized that I made some of the same decisions he did when he was my age.

To prevent my children from repeating this cycle of

mistakes, I am willing to endure the struggles that come with self-reflection or learning about my good and bad actions, which is why I love the way my wife has been my mirror of correction with love. She is strong enough to tell me what I need to hear and wise enough to tell me those things how I need to hear them in order to get me to respond with the desired change or improvement. It's tough sometimes, but God has given me the strength to endure and overcome.

I am committed to passing on to my children the actions of commitment, faithfulness, loving and valuing people more than things, displaying the highest level of integrity, being trustworthy, possessing a never-give-up mentality, a mindset to work beyond their mental wall of fatigue, a willingness to give to others in need, and a determination to be the best example they can be.

Of course, there are other things to be aware of, like a poverty mindset. I came from a life of struggle, and without being aware of the habits enforced by our own mindsets, our children have the potential to reproduce them more zealously than we did.

With my own children, we watched plenty of television early on when they were between the ages of two and thirteen and did not do enough reading, which hindered our ability to comprehend things beyond what someone else was saying. For me, this meant not understanding things as fast as others, which caused delays in my advancement in many areas. Too much television equals a loss of time and not enough attention for the things that will help us become better providers for our families or just be productive in life. I am not speaking against enjoying a good movie from time to time or watching your favorite sport, but I am referring to spending too many hours in front of a television.

The result of watching too much television can be that we have to tell a long story just to make a point; however, when we read a lot, it gives us the ability to make a statement that tells a story. We become more concise in our communication with others.

Another example of what can be passed on is spending money beyond our bank accounts, which is common today with a lot of people. I remember in the first few years of our marriage, I had to have money in my pocket even when we couldn't afford it. We couldn't afford to buy fries from a fast-food restaurant in the beginning. Yes, that is the truth! This goes back to understanding how we think and why we do the things we do in order to understand why it's so important to change our way of thinking and better our future.

One of my personal struggles was that I would go out and purchase chrome wheels for my cars without considering the expenses. With chrome wheels, you have to replace the tires more often because they don't last very long on those chrome wheels, and you lose gas mileage due to driving on larger wheels. I share this nugget of information because I see this often today with young folks spending almost five thousand dollars for wheels and tires for a look that only lasts about six months to a year. And, if you don't have the money to replace the tires yearly, the car gets parked because you can't afford to drive it based on decisions about wheels and tires. Now, there is nothing wrong with this if that's what you like and you can afford it, because some wheels do make the cars look better. Personally, I choose to save that money now or invest it into something that will increase in value.

Becoming a good steward of money is critical. Saving up for a rainy day or, better yet, being in a position to capitalize on a good investment opportunity is how we want to position ourselves.

When living in struggle, entertainment and laughter become extremely important even though these same things can be enjoyed when living a fulfilled life with peace of mind. This is heavily due to the fact that when we are in that place of struggle or living paycheck to paycheck, we don't see ourselves achieving much at all based on our environment. This is like having your dreams feel like a distant fantasy, never to be experienced up close and personal.

The one thing I have gone back to is seeing the value in the little things and appreciating those things that many people take for granted. I have learned that spending quality time with my family outweighs the value of any materialistic purchase I could ever make for them. Buying things is necessary sometimes, but spending quality time is priceless because it has a lifelong effect on the ones we spend it with.

Learning about my parents gives me a greater level of understanding and appreciation for them; I now realize they only did what they knew to do. I'm not making excuses for them at all because they willingly made some decisions they knew were wrong. However, I have a better understanding because now I know that some of the actions were a duplication of what they learned from their parents. I see great value in this assessment because it also helps me see where I am, define where I want to go, and then I can seek information that will help me reach my destination as a better decision-maker.

CHAPTER 38

Education Matters

First of all, "education" doesn't always mean we need to have a college degree—though in today's job industry, a degree can determine your salary as well as the type of job you receive. What I want to focus on is that while being educated doesn't make us any better than anyone else, it does put us in a position to make better decisions. However, we must be careful because knowledge can cause us to be puffed up and arrogant. Being arrogant can lead us to attack others with our knowledge instead of patiently feeding people the information and guidance they need to make better decisions themselves.

Getting an education can decrease our dependency

on others explaining things to us and may reduce the need to believe what others tell us, which could be their personal opinions about something and not the facts. Not being educated about things we are directly involved in can be dangerous. Sometimes, we find ourselves trusting and relying on folks who don't have our best interests in mind. This can lead us down a path of being manipulated, used, and abused by some heartless individuals, so we must study whether we are pursuing a degree or not because our future depends on it.

As a youth, I hated reading, but now, as an adult, I can't read enough to satisfy my hunger and thirst for knowledge, understanding, and wisdom. I am determined to become an auditory learner, or someone with the ability to just listen to a matter and clearly understand how something works after hearing the explanation. The other types of learners are visual learners, who need to see a picture or a demonstration of some kind, and hands-on learners, who need to put it together with their hands to understand it. We all use these methods to learn, but in order to become an auditory learner, we must read and study to improve our comprehension level so we can listen to something or read something one time, then turn around and explain or demonstrate it to someone else.

After getting an education, we must learn how to be patient with others who have not reached the same level of competence, keeping in mind the times when we didn't know or understand something. Education and knowledge are the doorway to understanding, which is the doorway to wisdom. I may have information but not understand how to apply that knowledge. I gain experience as I use information, and then, over time, I will make wiser decisions based on lessons learned. Thus, knowledge leads to understanding, and understanding leads to wisdom.

CHAPTER 39

Beyond My Internal Ceiling

After all of that, we still have to get beyond our internal ceiling, or our internal lid. As my son told me a couple of years ago, I was still restricted by the pain of my past and was not really enjoying life the way I should be. My youngest daughter basically told me to please stop talking for a moment and just listen. She was saying, "I need you, but in this moment, I just want you to listen." What these moments said to me was this is a season to just listen, learn, and enjoy life.

This season has been about staying in position long enough to see the hand of God at work in my life and having enough courage to accept the blessings of God when they show up.

You see, having that internal lid can cause us to reject Godly help when it comes our way. For me, that has been running from the big stage out of fear because I accepted the verbal lid put on me by my mother when she said that I would never be anything.

Now, I know that I am well beyond that statement as a man of many accomplishments, but I can honestly say that I haven't crossed the bridge yet into the fulfilling life God has set aside for me so that I may be a blessing to others.

The problem with having an internal lid is that we tend to look for roadblocks in our lives that don't really exist. We expect rejection or wait for someone to say no based on that internal lid. We tend to get ourselves out of position before the blessing completely manifests itself in our lives.

My message today is to stay in position long enough to see and receive the blessings of God. This requires going through a season of trusting God more than yourself, experiencing deliverance from a challenging situation to achieve success.

As for me, I had to decide that I wanted more out of life than just hearing someone say that I could be doing this or that, but I was holding myself back. So, instead of rejecting the blessings and removing myself from the position by self-sabotaging my own progress, I now stand in the established place of purpose with patience and allow God to do what He intended all along, which is to bless me so that I am positioned and equipped to bless others. Thank you, God!

The first step is to decide to go beyond our own imaginations and begin to believe and do the right things. Next, we must realize that we have made it beyond our pasts and pause and reflect on our journeys. Then, we can recognize the many gifts and blessings all around us. As a friend once said, we must slow down and see the signs that are all around us.

CHAPTER 40

In Conclusion

I believe that telling our stories is how we acknowledge what God has done for us and what He can do for others. Our stories are a reflection of the love, forgiveness, deliverance, grace, mercy, and purpose for our lives that He has shown to us through His Son and our Savior, Jesus Christ. As we tell our stories to others, we become living examples of the power of God and hope for those we share them with.

Sometimes, we reach what I call a defining moment, where we'll either do something that will cost us everything or we'll experience God's divine intervention and begin to follow the wise instructions of someone God sends our way. This is truly a sign that God's purpose for our lives is bigger than our imagination because God always supersedes our thoughts. What God has for us is for us, and no matter what anyone else says or does, they cannot stop the will of God for our lives. God's purpose for our lives never goes away, even with all the mistakes we make. He forgives us and even covers us when we don't deserve it.

As parents, we want our voices to make a difference in our children's lives, so we must work hard to keep the relationship intact if we want our children to respond to the instructions we give them during critical moments in life.

God will lead us to a place where we can only trust Him for deliverance, which I call the valley experience. It's where God exposed me to myself in order to help me understand how much I need Him and all the things that He is purging out of my life so that I may be more effective in His Kingdom. This includes every area of my life, from how I think to what I say to all that I do.

One area has been how I have made many decisions based on my emotions, and that usually doesn't have the outcome I truly want, nor is it the outcome that God intends. God gives us assignments, and sometimes we try to give those assignments to someone else, taking the back seat when God says to move to the front because He wants the people to see us, knowing that we will give Him the glory for what He allows us to achieve.

God's destination for us comes with a responsibility that we must accept. He has already given us everything we need to walk in our purpose. God has a platform for us that's in the presence of great men and women, so we must accept that He chose us for such a tremendous task and we must simply walk in it.

My Prayer

God, I ask for your forgiveness, and I thank you for giving me the strength to forgive others. I pray that this book will touch the lives of those in need of healing from within. I pray that your will is done throughout the earth and that others come to know your love, appreciate your grace, and embrace your mercy. Thank you for sacrificing your Son and our Savior so that we may have access to a better life. I pray that love and life will matter to all more than things that have no ability to embrace and encourage another. I thank you for everything you have done, everything you are doing, and everything you are about to do. You are greater than anyone could ever imagine, and all we have to do is accept, serve, and trust you. God, you are awesome. In Jesus's name, I pray. Amen.

The Power of Change

The winds blow, the seas rage
There are some forces we cannot cage
Rain falls and water flows
Where it ends, nobody knows
Fire consumes everything in its path
Cold weather has a relentless wrath
Change is a force like love and hate
We cannot stop its undeniable fate
We must adjust with the force of change
Or be consumed by its endless range

By Brian M. Darden Sr.

EPILOGUE

Next Chapter TBD

Sharing our stories within has the ability to liberate us as well as the capability to set others free each time we tell them.

With every tragedy, there is a triumph. With every challenge, there is a choice. And the decisions we make will determine our progress in life.

Writing has been a strong part of my personal therapy; I now realize that my purpose is greater than the pain of my past.

What I've learned along this journey of facing my internal reality is that there are two paths: we will either experience a controlled release of our hidden pain by telling our story incrementally, or we will experience an uncontrolled release of pain while reacting in a moment. If we let our pain build up inside, we could lash out at someone who may be completely unaware of our story within, and that someone could be an immediate family member, significant other, or someone else we deeply care about.

We make decisions every day based on our stories within, and our actions often go unexplained or tend to be misunderstood by most simply because they don't know anything about our backgrounds or why we are so guarded when interacting with others.

We silently communicate with others as a way of guarding ourselves or work extremely hard to deflect and defend against perceived attacks from others during conversations. This causes others to draw closer or move further away from us as a result of our actions.

I have been an overprotective father and husband because of my own experiences with unbelievable moments of struggle and abuse. These experiences are never pleasant, but they have a way of turning us into people of strength, able to endure and overcome adversity on any level.

I truly believe that God chooses certain individuals to do things that appear impossible to others. He prepares those people to lead others as an example of hope and become a real-life display of deliverance from some form of hardship or extreme adversity because most of us believe after seeing something accomplished by others.

I believe that to live life at our full potential, we must be relieved of the pain and internal restrictions from our stories within. Some of those places in our pasts have created a self-containing, mentally sustained box of limitations sealed by fear, doubt, and low self-esteem, but that box doesn't have to limit us forever.

Like a friend once said to me, we must know ourselves and understand why we make the decisions we do in order to properly plan and make sustainable progress in our lives and become a life of influence for others, near and far. We no longer try in life. "We Do."

About the Author

BRIAN DARDEN is a Newport News Apprentice School graduate with more than 35 years of shipyard industry experience. Currently, he is a dedicated servant leader within his organization. Brian has been married to Kimberly S. Darden for 33 years and counting, and together they have three adult children and seven grandchildren. Brian enjoys singing and encouraging others, and he is thankful to be a servant of God.

Made in United States
North Haven, CT
24 February 2025